Mother Most Powerful

Mother Most Powerful

Reflections on the Litany of Loreto

Marge Steinhage Fenelon

Our Sunday Visitor
Huntington, Indiana

Nihil Obstat
Msgr. Michael Heintz, Ph.D.
Censor Librorum

Imprimatur
✠ Kevin C. Rhoades
Bishop of Fort Wayne-South Bend
April 18, 2024

The *Nihil Obstat* and *Imprimatur* are official declarations that a book is free from doctrinal or moral error. It is not implied that those who have granted the *Nihil Obstat* and *Imprimatur* agree with the contents, opinions, or statements expressed.

29 28 27 26 25 24   1 2 3 4 5 6 7 8 9

Our Sunday Visitor Publishing Division
Our Sunday Visitor, Inc.
200 Noll Plaza
Huntington, IN 46750
www.osv.com
1-800-348-2440

ISBN: 978-1-63966-098-8 (Inventory No. T2827)
1. RELIGION—Christianity —Catholic.
2. RELIGION—Christian Theology—Mariology.
3. RELIGION—Christian Living—Prayer.

eISBN: 978-1-63966-099-5
LCCN: 2024940609

Cover and interior design: Chelsea Alt
Cover art: *Assumption of Mary*, Guido Reni (Wikimedia Commons/GoldenArtists)

PRINTED IN THE UNITED STATES OF AMERICA

For Mary's children who have deep devotion to her,
and those who wish they had.

For you, my Mother Most Powerful.
May this book be of help to you in drawing
those you love into the home of your heart.

CONTENTS

PREFACE

I have written several books on Marian devotion, but none like *Mother Most Powerful*. True, it is inspirational like my other Mary books, and it contains valuable information just as they do. It is filled with devotion and love for our Blessed Mother as all my works are. Yet this book has a rhythm all its own. Each reflection follows the same format and pattern, pondering one of the fifty-four titles of Mary in the Litany of Loreto. At the same time, each reflection is unique. The reflections build one upon another like an exquisite mosaic. Yet somehow and in some divine way they all work together. I hope that the cadence of the reflections gives you the feeling of a song of praise, because that is how I felt while writing them.

Mother Most Powerful stands apart from my other books in another way as well. My other books have generally looked at Mary from a single perspective. *America's Mary: The Story of Our Lady of Good Help*, for example, relays in narrative style the history and happenings of Mary's appearance to Adele Brise in the dense Northwoods of Champion, Wisconsin, in 1859. *Our Lady, Undoer of Knots* chronicles my trip through the Holy Land and places it in the context of the famous Marian novena. *Mother Most Powerful*, on the other hand, looks at Mary in fifty-four completely diverse ways! Each title of Mary in the Litany of Loreto has its own character, history, and meaning, making the writing of this book both a challenge and a delight. To be honest, I had never thought of Mary in so many ways, and, consequently, I learned far more about her than I expected in the writing of the manuscript. It was a little like the old adage, "Just when you think you've seen it all …" This time, though, I was grateful that I had not seen it all and found myself marveling at the dimensions and differences between each of Mary's titles.

The book you hold in your hands is meant to be both read and prayed. My goal was to offer content that would captivate your interest and imagination while at the same time leading you deeper and deeper into a prayerful relationship with our Blessed Mother. The reflections can be read and prayed in any order and in whatever frequency. You can use this book as your companion for a fifty-four-day Rosary novena (traditionally said with twenty-seven days of petition for a particular intention and then twenty-seven days of thanksgiving for the granting of the intention), as a fifty-four-day novena by itself, or you might prefer to take your time with it, making it last for weeks, months, or even over the course of a year. You can also use this book in a group setting, with the members reading the same reflections in the same sequence and then meeting to discuss the variety of impressions and inspirations for each of Mary's titles. The choice is yours, of course, as it is essential that you use this book in the way that is most fruitful for you.

I pray that, regardless of how you use it, this book will challenge you, invigorate you, and increase in you an ardent, lasting love for Mary. She most certainly and ardently loves you!

Marge Steinhage Fenelon

The Litany of Loreto

Lord, have mercy.
Christ, have mercy.
Lord, have mercy.
Christ hear us.
Christ graciously hear us.
God, the Father of heaven,
have mercy on us.
God the Son, Redeemer of the world, ...
God the Holy Spirit, ...
Holy Trinity, one God, ...

Holy Mary,
pray for us.
Holy Mother of God, ...
Holy Virgin of virgins, ...
Mother of Christ, ...
Mother of the Church, ...
Mother of Mercy, ...
Mother of Divine Grace, ...
Mother of Hope, ...
Mother most pure, ...
Mother most chaste, ...
Mother inviolate, ...
Mother undefiled, ...
Mother most amiable, ...
Mother admirable, ...
Mother of good counsel, ...
Mother of our Creator, ...

Mother of our Savior, …
Virgin most prudent, …
Virgin most venerable, …
Virgin most renowned, …
Virgin most powerful, …
Virgin most merciful, …
Virgin most faithful, …
Mirror of justice, …
Seat of wisdom, …
Cause of our joy, …
Spiritual vessel, …
Vessel of honor, …
Singular vessel of devotion, …
Mystical rose, …
Tower of David, …
Tower of ivory, …
House of gold, …
Ark of the covenant, …
Gate of heaven, …
Morning star, …
Health of the sick, …
Refuge of sinners, …
Solace of Migrants, …

Comfort of the afflicted, …
Help of Christians, …
Queen of Angels, …
Queen of Patriarchs, …
Queen of Prophets, …
Queen of Apostles, …
Queen of Martyrs, …
Queen of Confessors, …
Queen of Virgins, …

Queen of all Saints, …
Queen conceived without original sin, …
Queen assumed into heaven, …
Queen of the most holy Rosary, …
Queen of families, …
Queen of peace, …

Lamb of God, who takes away the sins of the world,
spare us, O Lord.

Lamb of God, who takes away the sins of the world,
graciously hear us, O Lord.

Lamb of God, who takes away the sins of the world,
have mercy on us.

Pray for us, O holy Mother of God.
That we may be made worthy of the promises of Christ.

Let us pray.

Grant, we beseech thee,
O Lord God,
that we, your servants,
may enjoy perpetual health of mind and body;
and by the glorious intercession of the Blessed Mary, ever Virgin,
may be delivered from present sorrow,
and obtain eternal joy.
Through Christ our Lord.
Amen.

INTRODUCTION

HISTORY OF THE LITANY OF LORETO

Of all the litanies to Mary circling the globe, the most used and well-known is the Litany of Loreto. Used at the Shrine of Loreto in Recanati, Italy, on every Saturday and every feast day of Mary, it was further popularized by the innumerable pilgrims who visited the shrine and carried the litany with them on their return journeys. From at least the fifteenth century, Loreto had become one of the most noted pilgrimage sites in the world because it enshrines three walls from the home in Nazareth in which Mary was born and in which the Annunciation and Incarnation took place.[1]

How it came to be that Mary's house — or part of it — came to Recanati from Nazareth has substantial bearing on the Litany of Loreto's widespread popularity and use. According to tradition, the house was carried away from Nazareth in 1291 by angels to protect it from Saracen invaders who were on a campaign to demolish all the Christian buildings in the Holy

Land. They had made it known that their next target was the house of Mary. On May 12, 1291, the house was miraculously moved, or translated, from Nazareth to Trsat in the region of Dalmatia (now part of Croatia). It was discovered by woodcutters and became a noted pilgrimage site. After some time, the house was again translated by angels to an area near the Port of Recanati, Italy, on the spot where a pagan temple once stood. In the forest, shepherds saw a dazzling light in the sky, and behind the light, the mysterious house. Unfortunately, the area was infested with dangerous bandits and so the house was again translated to higher ground on land belonging to the Antici brothers. Not understanding the full spiritual impact of the gift that had been given to them, the greedy brothers confiscated the pilgrims' offerings and kept them for themselves.

On the night between December 9 and 10, 1294, angels again moved the house, this time to yet higher ground in Recanati near a public road. The locals clearly understood the worth of the little house, and they gave it great care and veneration, even building a sturdy wall to protect it from the elements. This final resting place of Mary's house was a hill covered with laurel trees (*laurus* in Latin), and the place was called *Lauretum*, which later became known as Loreto. Between the fifteenth and seventeenth centuries, the Basilica of Loreto was built over the house to protect and preserve it.[2]

HONORED SINCE APOSTOLIC TIMES

Inside the House of Loreto are two artifacts that tell us much about how Our Lady was honored even in apostolic times, and why the Saracens were determined to destroy the house. The first artifact is a stone altar said to have been consecrated by Saint Peter and used for the celebration of the Eucharist in the early Church. The second artifact is a wooden statue of Mary said to have been carved by Saint Luke. Sadly, the original statue was destroyed by fire in 1921. Pope Pius XI immediately commissioned and installed an exact copy of the statue. Archeologists studying the house and its contents have shown that the three walls of the House of Loreto are made of the exact same materials as the Grotto of the Annunciation in Nazareth and, if transported back there, would fit exactly in the space in front of the grotto.[3] While its proper name is the House of Loreto, it has often been referred to as the House of Gold of Our Lady because each day at sunset the light turns everything to gold for a time. Among the countless pilgrims who have visited the shrine are many saints, including St. Francis de Sales, St. Charles Borromeo, St. Ignatius of Loyola, and St. Alphonsus Liguori.

Since its origin, the Litany of Loreto has been a life-stream through the Church, inspiring poets, artists, musicians, and builders. We see evidence of this in the vast array of masterpieces structured and named after various titles of the Blessed Virgin found in her litany.[4] Considering the history and content of the House of Loreto, it is easy to see how Our Lady's litany could have sprung forth from it.

HOW LITANIES CAME TO BE

The tradition of praying litanies can be traced back to the early centuries. They are modeled after biblical examples of public prayers, which included repetition of verses and were chanted in unison accompanied by musical instruments. The ones most widely known are the psalms, for example, Psalm 135:[5]

> Praise the Lord, for he is good:
> for his mercy endures forever.
> Praise the God of gods:
> for his mercy endures forever.
> Praise the Lord of lords:

for his mercy endures forever.

After the era of Roman persecution of the Christians, the faithful — including the pope and clergy — would process through the streets from church to church chanting litanies. Litanies were used in the liturgy from the beginning of Christianity, often to pray for the peace and welfare of the world, the Church, and other commonly held intentions. The Prayer of the Faithful in each Mass takes the form of a litany, as does the penitential rite in which we repeat, "*Kyrie Eleison* … *Christe Eleison* … *Kyrie Eleison*." In the time of Saint Ambrose, two litanies were recited on the Sundays of Lent instead of the Gloria. Even today, we recite the Litany of the Saints on special holy days such as Holy Saturday and the Pentecost vigil. It is also used during an Ordination Mass and when a bishop or church is consecrated. The custom of processing and chanting litanies became so popular that by the Middle Ages there were numberless variations of litanies (at least eighty that can be definitively counted), all honoring God the Father, the Son, the Holy Spirit, the Precious Blood, the Blessed Virgin, and various saints.[6]

The custom of praying Marian litanies, and specifically the Litany of Loreto, has its own historical path. According to Fr. Richard Klaver in his book, *The Litany of Loreto*, the Litany of Loreto is an outgrowth of Scripture and the writings of the Church Fathers. Some scholars believe it can be traced back to apostolic days. "And because Jesus loved her so, and honored her so, and called her Mother, the Church could do nothing less. So, it would be easy to compile a litany from the early liturgies and the writings of the Fathers of the Church."[7]

The custom of Marian litanies continued to grow, with many litanies originating in Ireland and carried throughout the world by Irish missionaries in the eighth century. As Fr. Klaver writes, some of the titles of Mary in these litanies included: "Sun of all maidens, Full Moon of beauty, Moon of generosity, Golden Apple Tree of the Three Persons, fragrant fresh branch, sea in flood-time, harp's melody, early sunrise, ripening corn, ocean of humanity, heart without sin, O Woman Friend, Virgin from the southern clime, Mother of the orphans, Rest of the infants, Mistress of the tribes, Ladder of Heaven, Queen of Life."[8]

CONTRIBUTIONS OF THE SAINTS

Saints as well have contributed to the custom of praying Marian litanies. For example, Saint Gertrude (1256–1301) composed a litany of Mary that expanded over time. At one point when Gertrude had learned that she was about to face a difficult trial, she became afraid. To allay her fears, Jesus gave her his own mother as hers. In a beautiful act of surrender, Saint Gertrude prayerfully offered herself to God and asked him what he wished of her. He told her, "Honor my Mother, who is seated at my side, and employ yourself in praising her." She then began to salute Mary using the titles, Paradise of Delight, Model of Discipline, White Lily of the Ever Peaceful and Glorious Trinity, Effulgent Rose, Delight of Heaven, Peerless Sanctuary of the Holy Ghost, and Radiant Rose of Heavenly Fragrance. She then went on to compose her own special litany of Our Lady, which in part read:

> Daughter of the Eternal Father, Spouse of the Holy Ghost, Virgin most glorious, most meek, gentle, sweet, compassionate, gracious; sweeter than the dripping honeycomb, Delight of the Holy Trinity, Temple of the living God, Shrine of the Holy Ghost, Glory of the Heavenly Jerusalem, never-failing spring of grace, Stream of everlasting life, Garden of heavenly Delight, Refuge of the sorrowful in spirit.

Some of these titles were Marian honors and titles adapted from other times and cultures.[9]

It is believed that the Litany of Loreto was compiled and published in Dillingen, Germany, in 1558 by St. Peter Canisius (1521–97). This is the first known written copy.[10] It seems that, during the fifteenth century, the Litany of Loreto was used as a processional prayer particularly for protection against calamities and devastation. It became so popular that it began to replace the Litany of the Saints in penitential processions. It soon became the most well-known Marian litany, and in 1587 Pope Sixtus V formally sanctioned the Litany of Loreto and attached to it a partial indulgence for Catholics who recited it fully.[11] The litany's prominence grew such that in 1597, Pope Paul V ordered it to be sung in the Basilica of St. Mary Major on vigils and feasts of Mary. This practice was the springboard for the Litany of Loreto to be generally adopted, being the only Marian litany approved worldwide for both private and public devotion. By this time, the numbers of litanies composed for various devotions had grown to such an extent that there was concern over possible abuses. Therefore, in 1601, Pope Clement VII forbade the public recitation of all litanies except the Litany of the Saints and the Litany of Loreto, although other litanies may be recited in private devotion.[12]

More important than its history and specifications, the Litany of Loreto is full of beauty and meaning for Christians. It is rich in both tradition and symbolism, with its fifty-four invocations lauding titles, attributes, and roles of the Blessed Virgin Mary in the plan of salvation. "In this work the whole Marian theology is briefly set forth, while at the same time the principal dogmas of our Faith and the moral duties of the Christian are brought to mind," Fr. Alexis Lépicier wrote in his book *The Fairest Flower of Paradise.*[13] To pray the Litany of Loreto is to give witness to our Catholic Faith and to proclaim the gifts of the

Mother of God, drawing her graces and favors upon us and those whom we care about. When we pray it, we join with the universal Church in a time-honored tradition that unites us as the People of God and children of Mary. Each invocation is a prayer itself, and together, the invocations become a song of praise for the power of God embodied in Our Lady.

Holy Mary

Lord our God,
when your Son was dying on the altar of the cross,
he gave us as our mother
the one he had chosen to be his own mother,
the Blessed Virgin Mary;
grant that we who call upon
the holy name of Mary, our mother,
with confidence in her protection
may receive strength and comfort
in all our needs. Amen.

Prayer from the Mass for the Holy Name of the Blessed Virgin Mary

The name *Maria,* or *Mariam,* appears to be the Greek version of the Hebrew name *Miriam.* We encounter this name only once in the Old Testament: It is the name of the sister of Moses and Aaron. Since Miriam and her brothers were born in Egypt, it is possible that the name might be of Egyptian origin.

The name *Moses* likely is Egyptian, since he was named by the daughter of Pharaoh, and there is no Hebrew counterpart for the name *Aaron*. If the name *Mary* is of Egyptian origin, then it means "the beloved one." The Hebrew name *Miriam* could be derived from either of two words: *marah*, meaning to be rebellious, or *mara*, meaning to be well-nourished. Both fit our Blessed Mother and give witness to her holiness.

Mary may not have been well-nourished physically, at least not in the way that we think of it today, but she certainly was well-nourished spiritually, since she was blessed among women and wholly devoted to God. The name *Mara* also points to Mary's beauty and perfection. Culturally, being well-nourished was synonymous with beauty and bodily perfection. In Mary's case this name would mean "the beautiful" or "the perfect one."[1]

As for the other possible meaning, given her complete adherence to God's will, it is hard to imagine Mary as being at all rebellious, but there are different kinds of rebelliousness. Consider how Mary is foreshadowed in the Book of Genesis:

> I will put enmity between you and the woman,
>   and between your offspring and hers;
> he will strike your head,
>   and you will strike his heel. (3:15)

Mary does not rebel against God, but rather against Satan, which is what is expected of all God's people.

The Church Fathers also attach a mystical meaning to the names of Mary's parents. *Joachim* means "preparation of the Lord," and *Anne* means "grace." Our Lord also bears a name with mystical meaning, as *Jesus* means, "for he will save his people from their sins" (Mt 1:21).

Mary's name has been cherished in the Church since apostolic times. Through the centuries, the Church Fathers and other spiritual writers have filled pages with praise for her Holy Name. Mary's name in and of itself points to her fullness of grace. Saint Ambrose said, "Thy Holy Name, O Mary, is a precious appointment, which breathes forth the order of divine grace." And Saint Bernard said, "In dangers, in perplexities, in every doubt, think of Mary, call on Mary: let her name not leave thy lips, let her not depart from thy heart." We see at the Annunciation that the Archangel Gabriel greets her as "favored one" or "full of grace," depending on the biblical translation.

Because Mary's holiness is all-encompassing, her very name is venerated. The feast of the Holy Name of Mary has been celebrated in the Church since 1513, when Pope Julius II granted an indult for the diocese of Cuenca, Spain. From there the devotion spread throughout Spain and beyond. In 1683, Pope Innocent XI established it as a feast for the universal Church in thanksgiving for the seemingly impossible defeat of the Turks by John Sobieski, newly crowned King of Poland, in the siege of Vienna. The feast is now celebrated annually on September 12, the day of Sobieski's triumph.[2]

REFLECTION

Because of her perfect holiness, we venerate the very name of Mary. And because Mary's name itself is holy, the Catholic Church has instituted a feast day in its honor. That is quite remarkable, since there is not another human person whose name is given such love and honor. Therefore, September 12 should be a special day for all of us, but so should every day that we utter the name *Mary*. What emotions, thoughts, and images does this name evoke in us?

PRAYER

O Mary, you are so holy that even your name is holy. There is no other human being like you, and I am grateful to be able to call you my mother. Let me always remember to venerate your name whenever I hear it and to use it spontaneously as a prayer for grace, protection, and direction throughout my life. Amen.

HOLY MOTHER OF GOD

Who doubts that the praises we give to the Mother of God redound to the honor of the Son of God; and, in like manner, that in honoring the Son we are also honoring the Mother?

St. Bernard of Clairvaux

The Council of Ephesus convened in AD 431 as a response to the heretical teachings of Nestorius, bishop of Constantinople. Nestorius objected to the title *Theotokos* (God-Bearer) that had long been used for the Blessed Virgin Mary. In his opinion, calling Mary Theotokos denied the divinity of Christ and therefore the title must not be used. Beginning on Christmas Day in 428, Nestorius preached a series of homilies arguing that Mary was not Theotokos, and many people were scandalized by it. It seemed to them that when Nestorius denied that Mary was the mother of God, he also claimed that Christ was merely a man who had been adopted by God as his son. The people sought the help of Saint Cyril, bishop of Alexandria, who immediately saw the dangers in Nestorius's teachings. Both parties appealed to Pope Celestine I, who then authorized Cyril to issue a series of anathemas, or ecclesiastical bans, against Nestorius. Nestorius stood firm in his heretical thinking and preaching and persuaded Emperor Theodosius to convene a general Church council — the Council of Ephesus. But the council did not favor Nestorius. Instead, it affirmed that the humanity and divinity of Jesus could not be separated, condemned the teachings of Nestorius, deposed him from his see, and formally proclaimed Mary Theotokos, the Mother of God.[1]

The council's proclamation made official what already had existed in the hearts of the faithful. From the early centuries, the feast of Mary, Mother of God, was celebrated in the Church. In 1974, Pope St. Paul VI made note of this and in his encyclical *Marialis Cultus* he wrote: "This celebration, assigned to January 1 in conformity with the ancient liturgy of the city of Rome, is meant to commemorate the part played by Mary in this mystery of salvation. It is meant also to exalt the singular dignity which this mystery brings to the 'holy Mother … through whom we were found worthy … to receive the Author of life.'"[2]

Of course, Mary was officially named "Mother of God" long before the Council of Ephesus and before the formal institution of the feast of Mary, Mother of God by St. Paul VI. Even before Jesus was conceived in her womb, the Archangel Gabriel appeared and told Mary that she would give birth to the Son of God:

> "And now, you will conceive in your womb and bear a son, and you will name him Jesus. He will be great and will be called the Son of the Most High, and the Lord God will give to him the throne of his ancestor David. He will reign over the house of Jacob forever, and of his kingdom there will be no end." Mary said to the angel, "How can this be, since I am a virgin?" The angel said to her, "The Holy Spirit will come upon you, and the power of the Most High will overshadow you; therefore, the child to be born will be

holy; he will be called Son of God." (Luke 1:31–35)

This proclamation was repeated during the Visitation, when Mary greeted Elizabeth. Enlightened by the Holy Spirit, Elizabeth proclaimed: "Blessed are you among women, and blessed is the fruit of your womb. And why has this happened to me, that the mother of my Lord comes to me?" (Lk 1:42–43). Elizabeth's Lord was God, and so her exclamation could mean only one thing: She recognized that Mary bore within her womb the Son of God, the Second Person of the Trinity, God himself.

REFLECTION

Elizabeth recognized Mary as the mother of God because the Holy Spirit moved her. We, too, can be moved by the Holy Spirit to recognize the mother of Our Lord. We may know that she is the mother of God because the *Catechism of the Catholic Church* says so. But knowing and sensing — as Elizabeth did — the truth about Mary's motherhood is different. To sense her as the mother of God means to sense her holiness, nearness, and place in our lives.

PRAYER

Mary, Mother of God, you have been given a title that no other human being can ever claim. It is a title of immense importance and responsibility. Yet you accepted it in complete humility and obedience. Help me, please, to appreciate your holiness, sense your nearness, and understand your place in my life. Amen.

Holy Virgin of Virgins

The Virgin Birth, indeed, was a new type of generation. As our mind begets a thought without in any way destroying the mind, so Mary begot the Word within herself without in any way affecting her virginity.

Venerable Fulton J. Sheen, *The World's First Love*

I laugh now when I remember how, as a child, I would insist that my "brain was hurting" as a form of rebellion against having to do homework that I found difficult to manage. I figured that, if I could convince my parents that the work was in some way harming my brain, they would let me get out of it. This childish antic gives rise to an important point. The challenge of the assignment in no way affected the matter of my brain! A thought does not harm or change the integrity of the brain; the brain remains intact, just as it was before the thought occurred. Thus the analogy Ven. Fulton Sheen gives in the above quote could be the foundation for a deep and lengthy meditation because it gives a human context to a divine mystery.

Never before and never since has there been a conception and birth like that of our Savior. That is why Fulton Sheen referred to it as a "new type of generation," and why his analogy is so effective. We read in the first chapter of the Gospel of John that God and his Word are one and the same. "In the beginning was the Word, and the Word was with God, and the Word was God" (1:1–2). Later John writes that "the Word became flesh and lived among us" (v. 14). When the Word was conceived in the womb of our Blessed Mother, it did not in any way change or harm the integrity of her virgin body. In our human understanding, this is impossible. But with God all things are possible.

That Mary was and remained a virgin before, during, and after Our Lord's conception and birth is a dogma (revealed truth) of the Catholic Church. There was no human seed involved, but rather it was caused by the power of the Holy Spirit, so that there could be no question that Jesus is the Son of God. Mary's preeminent faith and trust in God made her a willing instrument of the Incarnation and a prime example for all of us. Because of this, the Church teaches, Mary is the symbol and most perfect realization of the Church. "The Church indeed … by receiving the word of God in faith becomes herself a mother: By preaching and Baptism, she brings forth sons, who are conceived by the Holy Spirit and born of God, to a new and immortal life. She herself is a virgin, who keeps in its entirety and purity the faith she pledged to her spouse."[1]

REFLECTION

Mary conceived the Word within her womb, and the Word became flesh without involvement of conjugal relations, leaving Mary's virginity unchanged for all eternity. She was always completely pure, both physically and spiritually. She had no stain of original sin, and she had promised her virginity to God. Because of this she is the holiest among all holy virgins.

PRAYER

Mary, there is no other woman like you in all of creation. No virgin, no matter how holy, is as venerable as you are. You deserve all the honor and reverence I can give you, and yet I so often neglect to give you the honor and reverence you deserve. I stand numbly in the corner, not really knowing what to do. O Virgin of Virgins, call me to your side and allow me to experience your sweetness. Amen.

MOTHER OF CHRIST

At the first blow (of the scourging), I fell as if dead, and on recovering my senses, I beheld his Body bruised and beaten to the very ribs, so that his ribs could be seen.

As my Son was going to the place of his Passion, some men struck him on the back and others hit him in the face. And he was struck so violently and so brutally that although I did not see the person striking him, I distinctly heard the sound of the blow.

Our Lady to St. Bridget of Sweden

St. Bridget of Sweden (1303–73) received many visions from God throughout her life. Visions are considered private revelations and are carefully investigated by the Church before they are considered worthy of belief. They enlighten us about the lives of Christ, Mary, the saints, and the doctrines of the Church, but they do not belong to the deposit of Faith. For that reason, we are free to choose whether we believe them or not (see CCC

67). I choose to believe them, particularly those that come from acclaimed saints like Bridget of Sweden. She was a courageous woman who proved her holiness throughout her lifetime.

In one vision, Mary told Saint Bridget about her son's passion. Her words to Saint Bridget are difficult to read. While the Gospels give us vital eyewitness accounts of Christ's passion, crucifixion, and death, they fall short of the shocking details that would shake our hearts and help us understand the full extent of Our Lord's suffering. The Gospels relay the actions and teachings of Jesus; private revelations enlighten us about them.

What impresses me most about Our Lady's words to Saint Bridget is that they represent only a small fraction of the suffering that Christ endured physically, and that Mary endured emotionally and psychologically. Not only was Jesus' skin gouged by the scourging, but the torture left his ribs exposed. That means that no flesh remained on his back. Can you imagine the pain that that caused both Christ and his mother? If that were not enough, he was further beaten, and then the heavy beam of the cross was thrust upon him, digging into his exposed ribs. Finally, he was nailed to the cross and hung there in excruciating agony for three hours. What Christ and his mother withstood is incomprehensible to the rest of us.

Why did they do this? Because only Jesus could properly atone for our abominable sins. When Jesus asked the apostles who they and others thought he was, Simon Peter quickly answered, "You are the Christ, the Son of the living God" (Mt 16:16, RSV). "The word 'Christ' comes from the Greek translation of the Hebrew *Messiah*, which means 'anointed'" (CCC 436). Those who are anointed have been given a great mission. Jesus was given the singular mission of redeeming the world, and he accomplished that mission perfectly. Jesus is the Christ, the Anointed One, the God-Man who came to earth, experienced the human condition, suffered, and died so that we might live. On Pentecost,

Saint Peter preached to the crowds, calling them to repentance. He told them, "Therefore let the entire house of Israel know with certainty that God has made him both Lord and Messiah, this Jesus whom you crucified" (Acts 2:36). Jesus was anointed by his Father with the Holy Spirit, who is the anointing itself. Mary, too, was anointed since she carried the Christ in her womb and was given a singular mission in the plan of salvation. Mary, and only Mary, could be the Mother of Christ.

REFLECTION

Mary was the first to recognize Jesus as the Christ, the singularly anointed one who came to save mankind from damnation. Jesus was the first to recognize Mary as the Mother of Christ, the anointed one whose fiat made possible the coming of the Redeemer. Because of her surrender to God's will, Mary became part of Christ's mission and suffering, but she also became part of his victory over death and sin.

PRAYER

Mary, you were anointed to be the Mother of Christ and walked the path of victory with him. Walk along with me on my path toward heaven. Lead me to the victory that awaits me in eternity. Amen.

MOTHER OF THE CHURCH

Herein lies the reason why we, though unworthy and weak, yet in a spirit of trust and with ardent filial love, raise our eyes to her. She who once gave us Jesus, the fount of heavenly grace, cannot fail to offer her maternal help to the Church, especially at this time in which the Spouse of Christ strives with greater zeal to fulfill her salvific mission.

Pope St. Paul VI

The memorial of Mary, Mother of the Church, is celebrated on the Monday after Pentecost. This is fitting since at Pentecost Mary participated in the birth of the Church, when the Holy Spirit descended upon the disciples in the Upper Room. The Spirit came as the "rush of a violent wind" (Acts 2:2) that filled the entire house. Then tongues of fire appeared, resting on each of them, and they were filled with the Holy Spirit. In that moment, they were transformed, began speaking in foreign languages, and were filled with courage and zeal. After that, they headed out into the streets to proclaim the Good News and baptize (see Acts 2:1–13).

Mary was present at the birth of the Church, but her role began long before that. As a young maiden, she said yes to being the mother of God. When she said yes to that, she also said yes to being the mother of the Mystical Body of Christ. The term *Mystical Body* refers to all followers of Christ, in essence, the Church. The *Catechism* explains it this way: "By pronouncing her 'fiat' at the Annunciation and giving her consent to the Incarnation, Mary was already collaborating with the whole work her son was to accomplish. She is mother wherever he is Savior and head of the Mystical Body" (973).

Mary is the mother of the Mystical Body of Christ. Thus she is the mother of the Church. And who is included in the Church? We are. You, me, and every single one of the followers of Christ. She is our mother, and we are her children. Her mission and responsibility as Mother of the Church has been ongoing for thousands of years and will continue for all eternity. And so, we honor her under this special title and give thanks for her generosity.

Mary's title "Mother of the Church" is not to be confused with the title we give the Church itself: "Mother Church." This can be confusing, so let me explain. It is in the Church that we are born to new life through baptism, and that spiritual life is further nurtured and matured by the other sacraments. Generally, when we refer to the Church as "Mother," we are referring to the teachings, obligations, precepts, and laws of the Church. Just as a physical mother helps to feed, guide, protect, and educate her children, the Church does the same for the followers of Christ. We could not survive without her. As Mother *of the* Church, Mary also feeds, guides, protects, educates, and intercedes for us before her son.

REFLECTION

When we enter a Catholic church, we are entering the physical representation of Mother Church. The Church invites us to come inside and receive the graces and benefits she has in store for us. Within the Church we find Mary, who waits there for us so that she can lead us to her son. Mary is the person who draws us to Christ; the Church is the entity that does so.

PRAYER

Mary, Mother of the Church, my mother, teach me how to love Mother Church, to understand and embrace her teachings, to be courageous in living my Catholic faith, and help me grow closer to your son, Jesus. Amen.

MOTHER OF MERCY

Hail Holy Queen, Mother of mercy, our life, our sweetness, and our hope. To thee do we cry, poor banished children of Eve. To thee do we send up our sighs, mourning and weeping in this valley of tears. Turn then, most gracious advocate, thine eyes of mercy toward us. And after this, our exile, show unto us the blessed fruit of thy womb, Jesus. O clement, O loving, O sweet Virgin Mary.

When kings were consecrated in medieval times, their heads were anointed with oil. The oil was a symbol of mercy and reminded the king that, before all else, his reign should be one of kindness and beneficence toward his subjects. His primary occupation should be works of mercy, carefully balanced with prudent justice.[1] History tells us that not all kings lived up to their anointing. Some were greedy and cruel, and all of them were prone to human error. But there is one king whose reign is perfect and whose countenance is pure and merciful: Our Lord, Jesus Christ, King of the Universe. Jesus is mercy incarnate. All kings, therefore, should look to him as their model and guide.

Since biblical times, the mother of the king was known as the Queen Mother. It was not the wife of the king who sat on the throne beside him, but rather his mother. The Queen Mother helped him govern his kingdom and care for his subjects. If Our Lord is King of the Universe, and we know he is, then his mother, Mary, is Queen of the Universe. Our Lord was anointed to conduct his reign of mercy. So, too, Mary is anointed to conduct his reign of mercy. Jesus is not just a merciful king, but he is mercy itself, and so that makes Mary the Mother of Mercy.

As Mother of Mercy, Mary exercises compassion and pardon for sinners. St. Alphonsus Liguori said that the kingdom of God consists of justice and mercy, but Our Lord divided it. He reserved the kingdom of justice for himself and granted the kingdom of mercy to Mary, making her responsible for dispersing his mercy to mankind.[2]

Once when Mary appeared to St. Faustina Kowalska, she identified herself as Mother of Mercy. Saint Faustina wrote in her diary:

> Once, the confessor told me to pray for his intention, and I began a novena to the Mother of God. This novena consisted in the prayer "Hail, Holy Queen" recited nine times. Toward the end of the novena, I saw the Mother of God with the Infant Jesus in her arms. … I could not stop wondering at his beauty. … I heard a few of the words that the Mother of God spoke. … The words were: "I am not only the Queen of Heaven, but also the Mother of Mercy, and your mother."[3]

God's divine mercy is undeserved, unmerited, and often unsought, yet we receive it because of his infinite love for us. In his great wisdom, the Father has given us a tender and loving mother who desperately desires our salvation. She looks for every opportunity to fill our minds and hearts with God's mercy and rejoices when we accept it in humility. Just as a human mother offers mercy and compassion to her child before he even asks for it, Mary offers us mercy and compassion before we even ask for it. Indeed, she offers it before we even know we need it.

REFLECTION

It can be difficult to admit that we have faults and need mercy. It is easier to rationalize and justify our behavior than to admit when it is sinful and atone for it. At such times, our Blessed Mother, the Mother of Mercy, is there for us. She looks mercifully upon us and leads us by the hand to the feet of her merciful son so that we can repent, receive forgiveness, and begin again.

PRAYER

Mother of Mercy, you are the stream through which Divine Mercy flows. Your closeness to your son allows you to see my need for mercy before I am even aware of it. Help me, please, to always be aware of my need for Divine Mercy and to ask for it in complete humility. Amen.

Mother of Divine Grace

This is indeed a high point among all the gifts of grace conferred in the history of man and of the universe: Mary is "full of grace," because it is precisely in her that the Incarnation of the Word, the hypostatic union of the Son of God with human nature, is accomplished and fulfilled.

Pope St. John Paul II, *Redemptoris Mater*

In his *Summa Theologica*, St. Thomas Aquinas referred to Christ as the Author of Grace. He wrote:

> Faith and hope signify effects of grace with certain defects on the part of the recipient of grace, inasmuch as faith is of the unseen, and hope of what is not yet possessed. Hence it was not necessary that in Christ, who is the *author of grace*, there should be any defects such as faith and hope imply; but whatever perfection is in faith

> and hope was in Christ most perfectly; as in fire there are not all the modes of heat which are defective by the subject's defect, but whatever belongs to the perfection of heat.[1]

He further explained that, of all creation, Mary was nearest to the Author of Grace because she bore him in her womb. When she was conceived in Saint Anne's womb, she received the fullness of God's grace and later was given the privilege and task to distribute that grace. It then follows that, since Mary is Mother of God — the Author of Grace — she is the Mother of Divine Grace.

When I first heard the title "Mother of Divine Grace," I took it to mean only that Mary could distribute God's grace. Of course, that is true. But I came to realize that this title also refers to the fact that Mary is the mother of Christ, who is the Author of Grace. Mary is the mother of the source of all grace. No one can create grace but God himself. Mary cannot create grace. We simple human beings cannot create it, nor can the holiest of saints. Even though they were charged with spreading the Good News and performing miraculous works in the name of Jesus, the apostles could not create grace. Grace comes from God alone and is his divine gift to us for the sake of our salvation and happiness in eternity. We can pray for God's grace, we can accept God's grace, and we can allow it to influence us and govern our lives. Indeed, we rely on God's grace to survive on this earth, and we look to our Mother of Divine Grace to distribute God's grace to us.

REFLECTION

St. Bernardine of Siena loved Mary so much and was so grateful for the graces she showered upon him that he would offer her spiritual gifts and fast in her honor every Saturday. Every day he would go to a gate of the city of Siena called the Porta Camollia and there prostrate himself before a fresco of Mary. He understood the unparalleled dignity of our Mother of Divine Grace.[2]

PRAYER

Mother of Divine Grace, give me a heart like that of St. Bernardine of Siena. I so often forget to appreciate your position in the plan of my salvation and to show you signs of my love. Shower me with God's grace so that I may honor you all the days of my life. Amen.

Mother of Hope

When the wine gave out, the mother of Jesus said to him, "They have no wine." And Jesus said to her, "Woman, what concern is that to you and to me? My hour has not yet come." His mother said to the servants, "Do whatever he tells you."

John 2:3–5

The Wedding at Cana is one of my favorite Marian narratives from Scripture because it brings Mary's sensitivity to the foreground. Mary, as well as Jesus and his disciples, were invited to the wedding celebration of a young couple, perhaps relatives of hers. Mary must have been one of the most honored guests there, not because of her social position, but because she was so kind, joyful, loving, and loved. I imagine that the other guests were drawn to her simply because she radiated God's magnificence in every word, smile, gesture, nod, or blink of the eye. She was perceptive and ever attentive to the needs of others. So, despite the revelry and activity, she noticed that something was amiss. The wedding couple had run out of wine, and that would have been a major embarrassment for a first-century Jewish wedding party! In that time and place, wedding feasts lasted for days, everyone was invited, and it was the responsibility of the hosts to keep the guests well fed and their wine glasses filled. As an attentive friend with a mother's tender instincts, Mary noticed this and resolved to do something about it.

Mary did not have money or resources to obtain more wine, but she had a son who had the ability to perform miracles. So, she appealed to Jesus in hopeful expectation that he would help the young couple. She had trust in his divinity and hope in his compassion. I am most touched by the way Mary approached Our Lord and convinced him to help the wedding hosts in their predicament. She did not tell him directly that she wanted him to create more wine, nor did she try to coerce or dare him into doing it. In fact, she did not even ask him directly. Instead, she merely stated the fact: "They have no wine." Then she left the rest to him. Jesus' response is surprising. He calls her "woman" and asks her what this situation has to do with him or with her. He informs her that his hour has not yet come, meaning that it is not yet time for him to reveal himself as the Messiah.

Jesus had good reason for his response. His identity had to be kept hidden until the right time, and he had to be prudent about which miracles he performed and when. Mary was left with what appeared to be a refusal of her request, yet she continued to hope that Jesus would honor it. She said nothing more to Jesus but told the servants, "Do whatever he tells you," and left it at that.

Jesus indeed did honor Mary's request by changing six large jugs filled with purification water into wine. It was not just any wine, mind you, but the best wine the guests had ever tasted. It seems to me that at that moment Jesus was teaching us an especially important lesson about his mother. On a human level he wanted to honor and obey her, giving us the example of honoring our parents. On a divine level, he wanted to highlight Mary's intercessory power and hold her up as a genuine model of Christian hopefulness. During the wedding feast at Cana, Jesus revealed Mary as the Mother of Hope. Mary teaches us how to hope in Christ and, at the same time, is a supreme example of that same hope.

REFLECTION

As Mother of Hope, Mary wants us to hope in Christ as she did. Her hope extended from the miracle of changing water into wine, up the hill of Calvary, throughout the Crucifixion, and to the Resurrection. She brings us hope by interceding for us with her son, who will not refuse her requests.

PRAYER

O Mary, Mother of Hope, I so often forget that genuine hope lies in your son and in your gift of interceding before him. You are eager to present my needs and desires to him, and he is eager to grant your requests according to God's plan for me. Teach me how to be a person of hope. Be truly my Mother of Hope. Amen.

Mother Most Pure

Mary then is a specimen, and more than a specimen, in the purity of her soul and body, of what man was before his fall and what he would have been, had he risen to his full perfection.

St. John Henry Newman, *The Mystical Rose*

Forty days after Jesus was born, Joseph and Mary took him to the Temple in Jerusalem to present him to the Lord according to the Mosaic law. To the world, they seemed like an average Jewish family following the Jewish laws. But some, like Simeon and Anna, knew better. The child being brought to the Temple was the Messiah, and his mother was "full of grace," chosen from among all women. Jesus had no need to be consecrated to God, because he *was* God. Mary had no need for purification because she had been freed from the stain of original sin at her conception.

> When the time came for their purification according to the law of Moses, they brought him up to Jerusalem

> to present him to the Lord (as it is written in the law of the Lord, "Every firstborn male shall be designated as holy to the Lord"), and they offered a sacrifice according to what is stated in the law of the Lord, "a pair of turtledoves or two young pigeons." (Luke 2:22–24)

St. Thomas Aquinas explains that Jesus did not need purification and circumcision because he was not subject to the law. He submitted to the rituals to give an example of humility and obedience to others, and to remain free from calumny should the Jewish leaders try to make scandal of his not following the law. Because she was the Mother of God, Mary also was not subject to the law, but Our Lord wished her to follow the law for the same reasons. "Although the Blessed Virgin had no uncleanness, yet she wished to fulfill the observance of purification, not because she needed it, but on account of the precept of the Law."[1]

Mary was pure in every conceivable way: physically in her perpetual virginity; spiritually in her freedom from the consequences of original sin; mentally in her thoughts and perceptions; and emotionally in her actions and reactions. No other creature ever has been or ever will be as pure as the Blessed Virgin Mary. This is why we can undeniably call her Mother Most Pure.

Regarding Mary's purity, St. John Henry Newman wrote, "It was fitting, for [Christ's] honor and glory, that she who was the instrument of his bodily presence, should first be a miracle of his grace; it was fitting that she should triumph, where Eve had failed, and should 'bruise the serpent's head' by the spotlessness of her sanctity."[2]

REFLECTION

Imagine being so clean that you never had to bathe. It sounds ridiculous, right? Spiritually speaking, Mary was so clean that she never had to bathe. She remained pure in all ways, always. She never needed purification, never needed reconciliation with God, and never needed to make amends for anything she had done. Her purity is sublime and unparalleled, and we can only hope to strive to imitate her.

PRAYER

Mary, Mother Most Pure, I can never be as pure as you are, but I would like to strive toward that goal. Please stay near to me throughout my life and help me to be as pure as I possibly can be. Intercede for me before your son for the sake of my purity. Amen.

Mother Most Chaste

From these two spouses, who loved as no couple on earth has ever loved, learn that it takes not two to love, but three: you and you and Jesus.

Ven. Fulton J. Sheen, *The World's First Love*

My husband and I have been spiritual formators of young couples for many years. Our task has been to educate them on many facets of Catholic spirituality and to prepare them to live a holy life of consecration to the Blessed Virgin Mary. Together, we have written a curriculum that was broken up into units, each focusing on a different topic. One of the units was on chastity in marriage, a seemingly incongruous term.

At the start of the unit, we immediately had to explain that we were not referring to abstinence from sexual relations, although that can sometimes be temporarily necessary for periods of time. Nor were we suggesting that sex between a sacramentally married man and woman was in any way foul or sinful. Chastity, we told them, was not the antithesis to sexual relations, but rather an attitude toward one's own body and the body of one's spouse. Our bodies belong to God: They are sacred, worthy of respect, and should be cherished and kept pure. We find this attitude of chastity within marriage superbly demonstrated by Joseph and Mary.

In his book *The World's First Love*, Ven. Fulton J. Sheen called the marriage of Mary and Joseph "the world's happiest marriage." He pointed out that, while some marriages are based only on carnal ecstasies, others are based on the ecstasies of the spirit, as Mary and Joseph's were:

> It is one thing to give up the pleasures of married life because one is jaded with them, and quite another to give up the pleasures before they are ever experienced. Here the first marriage is of the heart and not of the flesh; it is a marriage such as the stars have, whose light unites in the atmosphere although the stars themselves do not; a marriage like the flowers in the garden in springtime, who give forth perfume, although they themselves do not touch; a marriage like an orchestration, where a great melody is produced but where one instrument is without contact with the other. Such a marriage was actually the type of marriage which took place between the Blessed Mother and St. Joseph, one in which the right to another was surrendered for a higher purpose.[1]

The fact that Mary had taken a vow of virginity long before she even met Joseph is of less importance than the fact that their union was formed for a higher purpose. They loved, cherished, and served each other in holy tenderness. They were chaste not only in body, but also in mind and spirit and in their respect for, and awe of, each other as God's precious creation. They kept themselves chaste in every way so that they could follow the will of God throughout their lives. True chastity is not only what we do with our bodies, but it also is what we do with our minds and spirits. To live a perfectly chaste life means to avoid anything that would lead our minds and hearts away from God. It means keeping our thoughts always upon God and never upon ourselves. It means holding nothing back and surrendering every part of our being and action to the Almighty.

This is how Mary and Joseph lived, and it was this attitude that allowed Mary to be mother and virgin at the same time. Before, during, and after the birth of Jesus, she remained constantly, totally chaste. She most certainly is our Mother Most Chaste.

REFLECTION

It is a great challenge to live a completely chaste life. Yet we all are called to follow the Holy Family's example, no matter what our state of life. We must be chaste in our thoughts, emotions, actions, and spirit, seeing ourselves and all others as precious creatures of God, worthy of love and respect.

PRAYER

Mother Most Chaste, I honor you as the perfect spouse of Saint Joseph and mother of Jesus. You lived a completely chaste life in accordance with God's will. Give me a chaste heart, Mary, so that I may always live in the spirit of chastity no matter where I go or what I do. Amen.

MOTHER INVIOLATE

When we have to offer anything to a great personage, we get it presented by the person he likes best, in order that the homage may be agreeable to him. So, our prayers have quite a different sort of merit when they are presented by the Blessed Virgin, because she is the only creature who has never offended God.

St. John Vianney[1]

Esther was a beautiful Jewish woman who found favor with the Persian King Ahasuerus. Enamored by her loveliness and charm, Ahasuerus took her as his queen. All seemed well until Haman, one of the king's assistants, used deceit and trickery to convince the king to destroy the Jewish people. Esther's adoptive father, Mordecai, was able to alert her to the impending danger for her people. He urged her to approach the king and plead with him to change his mind. In any other kingdom, perhaps this would not pose a problem for the queen. But Ahasuerus had leveled a decree saying that anyone who approached the king without first being called by him would be put to death. If Esther approached Ahasuerus without being called forth, she would be killed.

Despite the danger, Esther decided to approach the king anyway. But first she fasted for three days and prayed ardently to God for his mercy and protection over herself and her people. This has become known as "Esther's Prayer," and it is one of courage, humility, daring, and devotion. After praying, Esther approached Ahasuerus, who spared her life and promised to do for her whatever she asked. Bravely, Esther pleaded for her people, and Ahasuerus was so moved that he pledged his protection and care over the Jewish people. The king simply could not turn down the request of one who was so sincere and untainted (see Est 7–8).

Esther is a type, or prefigurement, of the Blessed Virgin Mary.[2] She demonstrated courage and confidence in petitioning the king on behalf of her people, even risking her own life to save them. Mary, too, is involved in the fate of her people — that is, all of us, since, through Christ, we all have become her people. She always has been and always will be involved in our fate. In her position as the heavenly queen, she goes before the King and pleads on our behalf. She is interested in our physical and spiritual well-being, and she intercedes in all our needs. Because of her purity, humility, beauty, courage, and daring, the King cannot resist calling her forth and granting her requests.

REFLECTION

Mary is inviolate, meaning that she is beyond reproach, respected, and cannot be attacked or destroyed. She is the only human person never to have offended God; she adheres constantly to his will and exists only to lovingly serve him. In her meekness and humility, she is strong, bold, and confident because she knows that her gifts come from God. Her perfection cannot be questioned, and the evil one can never attack or destroy her. Therefore, she is completely deserving of the title "Mother Inviolate."

PRAYER

Mother Inviolate, let me never fail to appreciate your irreproachable countenance and undivided devotion to me. Let me never forget that you are personally involved in my fate and will intercede for me before the King. Please give me the grace to be courageous, daring, and confident in living my faith. Amen.

MOTHER UNDEFILED

O my immaculate Queen,
Fair dove and the beloved of God,
Look on the many stains and wounds of my soul:
See me and have pity on me.
God, who loves you so much, denies nothing to you,
And you never refuse to assist those
who have recourse to you.
O Mother inviolate, pray for us.

St. Alphonsus Liguori

I was once in conversation with a woman who remarked on the frequency with which I went to confession. "I don't feel the need to go to confession very often. I guess I don't sin all that much," she said, chuckling. This happened at a time when I was receiving the Sacrament of Reconciliation on a weekly or biweekly basis because I was going through a particularly rough time in my life, so her remark was merited to a point. Although I knew it was meant in good humor, there was something about it that struck me negatively. "Impossible!" I thought to myself. "Every one of us offends God in some way every day." I had learned as a child that even the saints sinned, and, because of original sin, we are prone to offend God. The offenses may be so small that we are not even aware of them, but they are there all the same. That is, as the cliché goes, the human condition.

But there was one human being who indeed *was* exempt from the propensity toward sin: the Blessed Virgin Mary. Blessed Pope Pius IX explained this in his apostolic constitution on the Immaculate Conception, *Ineffabilis Deus*:

> We declare, pronounce, and define that the doctrine which holds that the most Blessed Virgin Mary, in the first instance of her conception, by a singular grace and privilege granted by Almighty God, in view of the merits of Jesus Christ, the Savior of the human race, was preserved free from all stain of original sin, is a doctrine revealed by God and therefore to be believed firmly and constantly by all the faithful.[1]

By a special grace of God, Mary never committed a single sin of any kind during her entire life on earth (see CCC 411). This privilege meant that she never fell into bad habits, never exhibited nasty behavior, and never experienced concupiscence. No one who knew her could find any fault in her. In all aspects of her being, thinking, speaking, and acting, she was completely and utterly undefiled. For me, this is completely unimaginable, not because I cannot fathom Mary's sin*less*ness, but because I am aware of my own sin*ful*ness. Sadly, I am aware of the sinfulness of other people, too.

Daily, we are surrounded with a multitude of temptations toward concupiscence. Entertainment, music, conversations, even books are filled with content that ranges anywhere from suggestive to lewd. We cannot escape it, yet that does not give us an excuse for paying attention to it. While Mary did not have the same technology or methods of communication in her day as we do today, she likely encountered situations and people through which she could have been defiled. However, she remained undefiled because of God's special grace. We are not privileged with that same grace, but we can pray for grace to avoid all defilement. And we most certainly can depend on our Mother Undefiled to accompany us, guide us, educate us, and intercede for us in our efforts to imitate her and avoid sin.

REFLECTION

How easy it is to participate in risqué conversations, let a foul word slip, watch sexualized content on television, or let our minds wander into areas they do not belong! This is the burden that we bear, the consequence of original sin that we must constantly resist. Yet God loves us and wants to help us in our weakness. To remain undefiled by temptation and sin, he wants us to look to Mary, our Mother Undefiled, for her help and prayers.

PRAYER

Mary, my Mother Undefiled, you did not experience the influences and temptations that I do. Still, you understand why and how I am affected by them. You understand because you know me better than I know myself. By your loving prayers, please help me to remain undefiled, through the grace of God. Amen.

Mother Most Amiable

There was a divine music in all that she said and did — in her mien, her air, her deportment, that charmed every true heart that came near her. Her innocence, her humility and modesty, her simplicity, sincerity, and truthfulness, her unaffected interest in everyone who came to her, her purity — it was these qualities which made her so lovable. And were we to see her now, neither our first thought nor our second thought would be what she could do for us with her son (though she can do much), but our first thought would be, "Oh, how beautiful!" and our second thought would be, "Oh, what ugly creatures are we!"

St. John Henry Newman, *The Mystical Rose*

In the above quote, St. John Newman is not demeaning human beings but rather demonstrating how far beyond us Mary is in terms of her qualities and holiness. We are worthy and beloved children of God, but we are not perfect in the way that Mary is perfect. His description of her paints a portrait of a woman who is lovable and loved by all, one who is amiable in all regards — not just amiable, but Mother Most Amiable.

I remember watching beauty pageants on television when I was a young girl. I was intrigued by the various competitions the contestants faced and eagerly awaited the awards at the end of the show. There was one that particularly kept me on the edge of my seat: Miss Congeniality. I was not much interested in the talent, beauty, or other awards. I was not even much interested in who received the crown and title. No, I wanted to know which one had earned the respect of the judges and other contestants as the most lovable among them. Miss Congeniality was the one who had a good relationship with everyone, was helpful to everyone, and was most liked by everyone. *That* is what mattered most to me. In my view, good looks and even talents go only so far in life and eventually fade away. But being congenial — amiable — lasts a lifetime. I think that if Mary were one of those contestants (highly unlikely, of course) she would be named Miss Congeniality. Her beauty would radiate, and her intellect and talents would astound, but her amiability would win the hearts of all.

There is evidence of Mary's amiability in Scripture. Consider the Visitation, when she hurried to the home of her cousin, Elizabeth, to help her with the final stages of pregnancy and subsequent childbirth. Although she had cares of her own, she set them aside in an act of true friendship, caring more for the elderly Elizabeth than for herself. Also consider the wedding at Cana, to which she, Our Lord, and his disciples were invited. She was such a part of the festivities that she noticed when the wine ran out. In her gentle, amiable way, she did what she could to solve the problem. Had she not been a lovable and respected guest, the servants would not have listened to her when she told them, "Do whatever he tells you" (Jn 2:5).

REFLECTION

It was not Mary's sinlessness alone that made her so dear to others; it was her pleasantness and way of winning others over. There are saints who were holy and virtuous, but none were as amiable and loved as Mary was. Mary was angelic and heavenly, and all who encountered her sensed this. Mary, our Mother Most Amiable, is irresistible to those who open their hearts to her.

PRAYER

Mother Most Amiable, I can only hope to strive to be as lovable as you are. I want to be amiable to all whom I encounter, but I so often am abrasive and inattentive to the needs of others despite my best efforts to avoid it. Show me how to be like you — gentle, humble, and amiable — so that I can be an example of Christ in the world. Amen.

Mother Admirable

Mother Thrice Admirable, Mother of Grace,
teach us our enemies bravely to face,
never regarding their number and might,
spreading your love over the earth's dark night,
so that the world through you made new,
pay to your son his homage due.

Fr. Joseph Kentenich

Jesuit Fr. Jakob Rem (1586–1618) was an instructor at the University of Ingolstadt in Germany who was honored for his holiness, wisdom, and exceptional intelligence. He lived in the university monastery and worked with the Marian Sodality there. The sodality's mission was to generate a great Catholic renewal, a mission that Fr. Rem embraced. In 1604, while the sodalists were singing the Litany of Loreto, Fr. Rem had an illumination that Mary's favorite title was "Mother Most Admirable." We should note here that the more recent translations of the Litany of Loreto use "Mother Admirable." Regardless, either version points to the fact that she is admirable above any of God's other creatures. Immediately after Fr. Rem's illumination, he had a vision that prompted him to instruct the choir to repeat that invocation three times, and this became the title under which the students venerated Mary. To them, she became the "Mother Thrice Admirable of Ingolstadt."[1] It is from Fr. Rem's illumination and his work with the Marian Sodality that Fr. Joseph Kentenich (1885–1968) adopted the title "Mother Thrice Admirable" in his work with the Marian Sodality at the Pallottine Seminary in Schoenstatt, Germany. The sodality eventually grew into the worldwide Apostolic Movement of Schoenstatt.

Illuminations are considered private revelations, and we are not obliged to believe them, even in cases where the Church has investigated the situation and found it to be worthy of belief. They do not belong to the deposit of faith and do not complete Christ's definitive Revelation, but they can help us live the Faith more fully (see CCC 67). Given Fr. Rem's reputation and the fruits of his work, I choose to believe his illumination — that the Blessed Mother gave him to understand that her favorite title is Mother Most Admirable. When we find something — or someone — to be admirable, we mean that they inspire in us approval, reverence, and affection, and that they are excellent and first-rate. We can never know whether Fr. Rem's illumination was meant only for the sodalists, or if Mary's preference for the title Mother Most Admirable was meant for all people of all time. Regardless, we see that this is an important title to her, and one we should carefully consider and contemplate in our prayer life.

In his acclaimed book *The Glories of Mary*, St. Alphonsus Liguori wrote an exclamation to Mary that fits the title "Mother Admirable":

> And thus, the saints, oh most sacred Virgin, marveling at so great splendor which surpasses the brightness of the sun, and the graceful loveliness of the moon, though

> they be the perfect flower and ideal of all beauty and considering the acclamations that burst forth from the heavens, never ceased to admire thy beauty, and do nothing but exclaim, and extol thee also, with acclamations of wonder and amazement.[2]

REFLECTION

Who is the most admirable person you know? What makes him or her admirable to you? Sometimes we find someone admirable without understanding why we feel that way. But with Mary, it is different. The list of reasons for which we could (and should) find her admirable is endless. Spending time contemplating that list of reasons will help us to grow closer to our Mother Admirable.

PRAYER

O Mother Admirable, I tend to admire people who are not spiritually wholesome or for the wrong reasons. You alone are worthy of true admiration. Please instill in my heart holy admiration for you and all that you have done in the plan of salvation. Amen.

MOTHER OF GOOD COUNSEL

A shoot shall come out from the stump of Jesse,
and a branch shall grow out of his roots.
The spirit of the LORD *shall rest on him,*
the spirit of wisdom and understanding,
the spirit of counsel and might,
the spirit of knowledge and the fear of the LORD.
His delight shall be in the fear of the LORD.

Isaiah 11:1–3

Counsel is one of the seven gifts of the Holy Spirit, all of which are found in Scripture. Together, they are wisdom, understanding, counsel, fortitude, knowledge, piety, and fear of the Lord. Christ possesses all of them in their fullness, and we, as his followers, must pray for them in abundance. They complete and perfect our virtues, making us docile and ready to obey divine inspiration (see CCC 1831).

When we hear the word *counsel*, we likely think about broken marriages and troubled families or individuals who go to a counselor to sort things out. Or we might think about a legal case in which counsel represents the person being tried for a crime. But scriptural counsel is different in that its purpose is to make us meek and humble like Our Lord — the ultimate Counselor. During Advent and Christmas each year, we hear the words of the Prophet Isaiah:

> For a child has been born for us,
> a son given to us;
> authority rests upon his shoulders,
> and he is named
> "Wonderful Counselor, Mighty God,
> Everlasting Father, Prince of Peace." (Isaiah 9:6)

Jesus is indeed a wonderful counselor and the source of all holy, genuine counsel. It is from Jesus' example that we have the evangelical counsels of poverty, chastity, and obedience. Commonly, those in consecrated life make vows to live the counsels in imitation of Our Lord. Some laity, such as my husband and myself, belong to apostolic communities who make a solemn promise to live in the spirit of the evangelical counsels according to their state of life. Regardless of the path we have chosen, all the faithful are called to live the evangelical counsels in imitation of the Wonderful Counselor, heeding his words and living by his example.

In his book *The Fairest Flower of Paradise*, Cardinal and Servite Father Alexis Lépicier wrote, "Next to Jesus, Mary is that privileged creature which possessed in a superlative degree the gift of counsel."[1] As Mary is a perfect human being, free of the effects of original sin, we can expect that she, like Jesus, has the gift of perfect counsel. Think again to the wedding at Cana when Mary asked Jesus to somehow fix the wine situation. The wedding couple had run out of wine — a terrible embarrassment to the couple and insult to the guests in that time and place — and Mary sought a solution. After asking her son for help, Mary counseled the servants to "do whatever he tells you." She knew that the wisest thing to do was to turn things over to Jesus and encourage everyone to follow his lead.

That is true for us today as well. When we are in a quandary, the best thing to do is to run to Our Lady and ask her counsel. She will guide us through our uncertainty, pointing always to the example and will of Our Lord. When we are confused, she will help to make things clear. When we are brokenhearted, she will heal our wounds. When we are defeated and exhausted, she will show us the next step. From the smallest detail of our lives to the largest milestone, she will counsel us perfectly because she is our Mother of Good Counsel.

REFLECTION

When we are faced with a difficult or confusing situation, our inclination is either to power through on our own or seek the opinions of others. That may be somewhat helpful, but it is not the complete solution. The real, lasting solution lies in the guidance of our Mother of Good Counsel, who works side by side with the Wonderful Counselor, our Lord Jesus Christ.

PRAYER

Mary, Mother of Good Counsel, I can be so stubborn at times. I often am too proud to admit I do not have the solutions to my problems. Sometimes I am too weak and confused to continue. Teach me meekness and humility so that, when faced with adversity, I will run to you and Jesus for counsel. Amen.

Mother of Our Creator

Thus, the heavens and the earth were finished, and all their multitude. And on the seventh day God finished the work that he had done, and he rested on the seventh day from all the work that he had done. So, God blessed the seventh day and hallowed it, because on it God rested from all the work that he had done in creation.

Genesis 2:1–3

Whenever I hear the creation story, I picture the Creator as God the Father. I can see beside him Jesus and the Holy Spirit, but the action — the actual creating — comes from the Father. This, of course, is theologically incorrect since the Father, Son, and Holy Spirit are Three in One and cannot be separated. The *Catechism* tells us:

The Trinity is One. We do not confess three Gods, but

> one God in three persons, the "consubstantial Trinity." The divine persons do not share the one divinity among themselves but each of them is God whole and entire. "The Father is that which the Son is, the Son that which the Father is, the Father and the Son that which the Holy Spirit is, i.e., by nature one God." In the words of the Fourth Lateran Council (1215): "Each of the persons is that supreme reality, viz., the divine substance, essence or nature." (253)

So it's true, the Father is the Creator in the creation narrative, but so are the Son and the Holy Spirit! The Three are inseparably One.

Now let us consider how this relates to Mary's divine maternity. If Mary is the mother of the Son, who is inseparable from the Father and the Holy Spirit, then she is the Mother of God (which we know from Scripture, from tradition, the saints, and from the Magisterium of the Church). If God is the Creator who created us (and all the world), then Mary is the Mother of Our Creator.

Perhaps this seems like an unnecessary dissection of a primary truth of the Faith, but there is reason for my madness. If all the above is true (and we know it is), then there is one more conclusion to be drawn. Since Mary is the Mother of God, then she is mother of her own creator. By human standards, that is impossible. Imagine being your father's mother. You would be obliged to honor and obey the very person to whom you gave birth. Yet, in essence, that is the position Mary was in. And she filled her role with grace, humility, and subservience. She alone, above all women, was given the privilege of being Mother of Our Creator.

As St. Louis de Montfort wrote:

> The Father has not given, and does not give, his Son except by her. He has no children but by her and communicates no graces but through her. The Son has not been formed for the whole world in general, except by her; and he is not daily formed and engendered except by her, in union with the Holy Ghost; neither does he form the members of our Lord's Mystical Body, except by her; and through her alone does he dispense his favors and his gifts.[1]

REFLECTION

The title "Mother of Our Creator" should fill us with both gratitude and awe. We should be grateful for Mary's purity, humility, and "yes" to becoming the mother of Christ — our creator. We should be in awe that any human being should have the unparalleled privilege of playing such a role in the economy of salvation.

PRAYER

Mary, Mother of Our Creator, my mother, thank you for agreeing to take on the astounding responsibility of giving birth to Jesus. Help me always to remember the unparalleled privilege you have received and to give you the honor you deserve. Amen.

MOTHER OF OUR SAVIOR

By his glorious Cross Christ has won salvation for all men. He redeemed them from the sin that held them in bondage.

CCC 1741

Along with Mary and her cousin Elizabeth, Saint Joseph was among the first to know the identity of the child Mary bore within her womb. The situation was a complicated one, however, as Mary had conceived the child before she and Joseph — her betrothed — were fully married and without their having had marital relations. The Gospel of Matthew tells us that Joseph was a righteous man and did not want to publicly disgrace Mary. So, he decided to quietly dismiss her from their marriage contract. Clearly, he loved her deeply and did not want to scandalize her, even though it appeared that she had been unfaithful to him. That is when God, in his infinite wisdom, intervened by sending an angel to Joseph in a dream to reveal the truth about Mary's pregnancy.

> An angel of the Lord appeared to him in a dream and said, "Joseph, son of David, do not be afraid to take Mary as your wife, for the child conceived in her is from the Holy Spirit. She will bear a son, and you are to name him Jesus, for he will save his people from their sins. All this took place to fulfill what had been spoken by the Lord through the prophet:
>
> > "Look the virgin shall conceive and bear a son,
> > and they shall name him Emmanuel." (Matthew 1:23)

Thus the child Mary bore was no ordinary child but Emmanuel, God with Us, the Savior of the World. This child named Jesus had come to save his people from their sins.

From that point on, Jesus was recognized as the Savior by those who had faith in God. Upon Jesus' birth, an angel suddenly appeared to the shepherds of Bethlehem as they watched their flocks in the fields. He told them, "Do not be afraid; for see — I am bringing you good news of great joy for all the people: to you is born this day in the city of David a Savior, who is the Messiah, the Lord" (Lk 2:10–11). The Magi had been studying the prophecies and followed the star in search of the Messiah. Simeon and Anna recognized the Savior when the Holy Family went to the Temple forty days after Jesus' birth. The apostles recognized the Savior when he called them to follow him. The Samaritan woman recognized the Savior when she met him at the well. The centurion recognized the Savior when he witnessed the earthquake and ominous marvels that occurred after Jesus surrendered his spirit to the Father. These are only a handful of examples in which Jesus — the child born in Bethlehem — was revealed as the Savior of the World.

Mary knew all along that which had to be revealed to others.

She bore the Savior in her womb, gave birth to him, nurtured him, taught him, shared her home with him, accompanied him in his ministry, and, finally, witnessed his gruesome death on the cross. Surely, it was an extraordinary joy to raise the Son of God. But also, it surely must have been a burden to have some sense of the suffering that lay ahead for both her son and herself. However, there is another aspect of this to consider. The Savior rose in glory on the third day. He had defeated death, crushed Satan, and redeemed all mankind. Mary not only witnessed this but was a part of it. The Savior's victory also is Mary's victory, because she is Mother of the Savior.

REFLECTION

Waiting for an inevitable misfortune can be a terrible burden. It can be difficult to concentrate on the present when one dreads the future. To continue in such adverse circumstances requires immense trust in Our Lord and a surrender of self-will. Even more, it requires pronounced faith in the Savior's ability to turn our crucifixion into a resurrection.

PRAYER

Mary, I know in my mind that you are Mother of the Savior, but I do not always feel it in my heart. Come close to me, please. Reveal to me the full meaning of this title and the impact it has on my life and the lives of my loved ones. Amen.

Virgin Most Prudent

Does not wisdom call,
and does not understanding raise her voice?
On the heights, beside the way,
at the crossroads she takes her stand;
beside the gates in front of the town,
at the entrance of the portals she cries out:
"To you, O people, I call,
and my cry is to all that live.
O simple ones, learn prudence;
acquire intelligence, you who lack it."

Proverbs 8:1–5

Prudence is one of the four cardinal virtues — the virtues that play a pivotal role in our spiritual well-being. The other three cardinal virtues are justice, fortitude, and temperance. Prudence, according to the *Catechism*, disposes practical reason, allows us to discern what is genuinely good in every circumstance, and assists us to choose the right means of achieving it. Prudence guides our conscience and helps us to apply moral principles to the situations in our lives (CCC 1805–1806). St. Thomas Aquinas succinctly describes prudence as "right reason applied to action" and says that prudence commands the other virtues and helps them reach their ends.[1]

The biblical Book of Proverbs refers to wisdom personified, but it could just as well refer to Mary. She takes her stand beside her son and calls out to all of us, adjuring us to be simple of heart, strive for intelligence, and learn prudence. Because she did not bear the consequences of original sin, she always enjoyed the perfect use of reason. Therefore, everything that she did was done with prudence. Our Lady spent her whole life following the will of God and doing her best to serve him. She belonged to him and considered herself his handmaid (see Lk 1:38). She exercised prudence in all things. She was prudent in the way she dressed, ate, and slept. She was prudent in the activities she undertook and the company she kept. She was prudent in her thoughts and words.

We see examples of Mary's prudence many times in the Scriptures. When the Bethlehem shepherds told Mary and Joseph what they had learned from the angel, Mary was careful in her reaction. Rather than bragging about her Savior-Son, she kept quiet and "treasured all these words and pondered them in her heart" (Lk 2:19). When she wanted to warn Jesus about the impending danger of those plotting against him, she did not burst into the house in which he was preaching and healing. Instead, she remained outside, allowing him the freedom to conduct his ministry as was necessary. During the entire passion and death of Our Lord, she resisted the temptation to interfere or cause a scene, choosing to proceed in humble subservience to God's will.

Mary wants the same for us as we make decisions according to our state of life. She is there to gently guide us in the way that is most prudent in the way we think, act, and choose, even in our dress, eating, sleeping, and the company we keep. As Saint Thomas explains, prudence applies universal principles to practical matters and actions.[2] In other words, prudence is the virtue that helps us choose the morally right action in any given situation. Mary not only lived this virtue, she exemplified it throughout her life.

REFLECTION

Sometimes we do not recognize when we are being imprudent because we justify our actions and decisions based on irrational and selfish standards. By studying Mary's example and relying on her motherly care, we can learn to exercise the virtue of prudence each day by choosing to do what we know to be right, striving to follow God's counsel and holy will for us. Mary, Virgin Most Prudent, will teach us how to practice this important virtue in all circumstances.

PRAYER

Virgin Most Prudent, you conquered that which I have yet to tackle. You remained prudent throughout your life, always acting in accord with right reason. Teach me, please, how to be as prudent as you are so that in all things I can listen carefully to God, discern his will for me, and follow his counsel. Amen.

Virgin Most Venerable

When they met her, they all blessed her with one accord and said to her, "You are the glory of Jerusalem, you are the great boast of Israel, you are the great pride of our nation! You have done all this with your own hand; you have done great good to Israel, and God is well pleased with it. May the Almighty Lord bless you forever!" And all the people said, "Amen."

Judith 15:9–10

On multiple occasions, I have been attacked for my devotion to Mary. The attacks always come from people who mistakenly think Catholics worship Mary and that we dishonor Jesus by being devoted to his mother. They think that our statues, images, and rosaries are idol worship, tools of Satan. They think that when we petition Mary, we are putting her on the same level as God or perhaps even above him. That could not be further from the truth.

Catholics do not worship Mary. Worship is for God alone, and anything outside of that is sacrilege. Catholics *venerate* Mary. There is a difference. Veneration is the act of giving honor and recognizing the dignity, high position, and importance of someone or something. We venerate Mary because of her perfection, holiness, closeness to God, and because she is the mother of Our Lord. When we venerate Mary (and other saints), we give glory to God and express "hope for some part and fellowship with them" (CCC 1090). We long to imitate them and grow in holiness so that we can enjoy eternity with God in heaven. If venerating Mary gives glory to God for his marvelous creation, then it is impossible for it to offend or dishonor Jesus.

St. Louis de Montfort explained this in *True Devotion to Mary*:

> If then, we establish solid devotion to our Blessed Lady, it is only to establish more perfectly devotion to Jesus Christ, and to provide an easy and secure means for finding Jesus Christ. If devotion to Our Lady removed us from Jesus Christ, we should have to reject it as an illusion of the devil; but so far from this being the case, devotion to Our Lady is, on the contrary, necessary for us — as I have already shown, and will show still further hereafter — as means of finding Jesus Christ perfectly, of loving him tenderly, of serving him faithfully.[1]

Mary's superb qualities and position in heaven give us reason to venerate her.

"The dignity of Mother of God to which Mary was elevated, and the office of Mother of men, which Jesus Christ confided to her, afford so many motives for us to honor the Holy Virgin with an especial cultus," wrote Cardinal Lépicier.[2] A *cultus* (or cult) in Catholic theology is a form of devotion, liturgical rite, or practice of veneration, not to be confused with secular, sometimes demonic, cults that use psychological and emotional manipulation to control others. Mary never manipulates or controls. Her only desire is to lead us closer to Jesus.

Veneration of Mary is necessary and life-giving for all of us. It provides us with a rich opportunity to have a deep and lasting relationship with a mother who loves beyond bounds, and who will care for her children beyond all measure, leading us into an ever-deeper relationship with her son.

REFLECTION

We can never love Mary enough. Why else would Jesus have given her to us as our mother as he hung dying on the cross? He loves us so much that he was willing to suffer and die for us, and even in his suffering he still wanted to do more for us. So he gave us his perfect mother to be our mother and to help us stay close to him even in our suffering. She is the Virgin Most Venerable because God chose her to be his own mother, and he wants us to stay close to her, trusting that she is truly our mother, too.

PRAYER

Virgin Most Venerable, I am sorry for any times I have not given you the honor you deserve. I want to learn to venerate you so that I can glorify God by my devotion to you. Pray for me, please, to have the grace to truly venerate you. Amen.

Virgin Most Renowned

The way of the righteous is level;
O Just One, you make smooth the path of the righteous.
In the path of your judgments,
O Lord, we wait for you;
your name and your renown
are the soul's desire.
My soul yearns for you in the night,
my spirit within me earnestly seeks you.
For when your judgments are in the earth,
the inhabitants of the world learn righteousness.

Isaiah 26:7–9

In our present times, the word *renowned* is frequently used regarding a person who is famous and, in some way, successful. Entrepreneurs, celebrities, sports teams, media franchises, social media influencers, and the like all have their fan bases —

some larger than others — who follow and gush over what they do. These groups and individuals have worked hard to win the hearts of their followers. They are famous because the world has noticed what they do. Our challenge as Christians is to discover and follow celebrities with moral character, whose work is edifying and uplifting.

Scripture offers us some prime examples of famous people worthy of following. Adam and Eve were the first two people of the world, the original parents of every person who has ever lived. Even though they committed the original sin, they became instrumental in God's plan of salvation. Noah is famous for building the Ark and saving his family and representatives of each kind of animal from the Flood. Abraham is our father in faith, and from him sprang a great nation. We have Moses to thank for receiving the Ten Commandments from God and for leading the Israelites out of slavery in Egypt. We remember David's stand against the giant, Goliath, killing him with his slingshot. Elijah is one of Israel's greatest prophets and is noted for his epic battle against the demon Baal. At the end of his life, he ascended to heaven in a fiery horse-drawn chariot. And Isaiah's eloquent verses bring inspiration and consolation to those who read and pray with them. The Bible is filled with outstanding characters who — for better or worse (think of Jezebel) — have left their mark on salvation history.

But there is one character who left her mark on the world, particularly on salvation history, who rises above any modern or biblical character: Mary. No single person has had as much impact on the course of history as the Blessed Virgin, and no heavenly being (aside from God) has as much impact on the world today. Nor will any creature (aside from God) have as much impact on civilization in the years to come as Our Lord's mother, the Virgin Most Renowned. Free of sin, uniquely chosen to be Mother of the Redeemer, and completely obedient to God, Mary is singular in her privileged position as Advocate, Helper, Benefactress, and Mediatrix (see CCC 969). St. Alphonsus Ligouri wrote: "Mary is, then, called omnipotent in the sense in which it can be understood of a creature, who is not capable of any divine attribute. She is omnipotent because she obtains by her prayers whatever she wishes."[1]

Our Blessed Mother, in a sense, is a celebrity who is noted for her (heavenly) success and has worked hard to win the hearts of her followers. Her fan base is made up of children of God who love her and want to live more holy and fulfilling lives. They follow all that she does so that they can imitate her and enter heaven at the end of their earthly lives. While the celebrities we see in the media are renowned according to the world's standards, Mary is renowned according to God's standards.

REFLECTION

Mary indeed is renowned because of the privileges that God has granted to her. Paradoxically, she is little known in many places because there are so many who do not appreciate or accept her. It is our task, then, to reclaim Mary's renown and extol her to the world.

PRAYER

Virgin Most Renowned, I know so much about famous people of today, but I know so little about you. Grant me the hunger to know more about you and the compulsion to extol you to the world. Amen.

Virgin Most Powerful

You have a mighty arm;
strong is your hand, high your right hand.
Righteousness and justice are the
foundation of your throne;
steadfast love and faithfulness go before you.

Psalm 89:13–14

The Prophet Ezekiel was granted a spectacular vision in which he felt the hand of the Lord upon him and saw a valley that was full of dry bones. God led Ezekiel all around the bones and then asked him whether the bones could live. Puzzled, Ezekiel turned the question back to God, claiming that only he would know. Then God commanded Ezekiel to prophesy to the bones and tell them that he would cause them to be restored and live again. When the prophet did as he had been commanded, he heard a tremendous rattling. The bones came together, flesh grew upon them, and they stood in the valley. God further instructed Ezekiel to command the renewed bones to breathe again, and they did. There before the prophet stood a vast multitude of people who had been brought back to life by Ezekiel's words and God's power (see Ez 37:1–10).

I love this scene from the Bible because it demonstrates how God can exercise his amazing power through even the simplest of creatures. Ezekiel was a mere human being, unremarkable and powerless. Yet God used him in a most miraculous way by creating a scene that defied all human understanding. Dead, dry bones coming back to life is not something you see every day. In fact, it is not something you see *any* day! But God did this through Ezekiel to prove to the prophet that he is All-Mighty, All-Knowing, and All-Powerful. God can do anything in and through any of his creatures. He need only say the word and it becomes reality.

So, when God created a child in the womb of Saint Anne, he had the ability to instill in that child a gift and mission that excelled any other mere human being. At the Father's bidding, this child became the mother of his Son, and he gave her the unique power to rule over his heart. Furthermore, he gave her the great mission to reign as queen over heaven and earth, to grant miracles, and to distribute his graces as she desired. The child's name was Mary.

> This is why the Blessed Virgin is called powerful — nay, sometimes all-powerful, because she has, more than anyone else, more than all angels and saints, this great, prevailing gift of prayer. No one has access to the Almighty as his mother has; none has merit such as hers. Her Son will deny her nothing that she asks, and herein lies her power. While she defends the Church, neither height nor depth, neither men nor evil spirits, neither great monarchs, nor craft of man, nor popular violence can avail to harm us; for human life is short, but Mary reigns above, a queen forever.[1]

Aside from Our Lord Jesus himself, no other creature can pray as purely or intercede as effectively with God as Mary. Aside from Jesus, no other creature is as fierce against the devil and his minions or as strong against temptation as Mary. No other woman who has given birth can claim to be both a virgin and a mother. Only Mary can. That is because she is the Virgin Most Powerful.

REFLECTION

Mary is powerful, but not in the same way God is powerful. She has power over our hearts because she loves us and because Jesus has charged her with the responsibility of helping us get to heaven. She can and will rescue us from temptation and the influences of evil. We need only call on her in our moments of distress.

PRAYER

Virgin Most Powerful, you can intercede for me before your son and protect me from Satan's wiles and trickery. Help me to remember to call upon you when I am in physical or spiritual danger. Help me to trust in the power God has given you. Amen.

Virgin Most Merciful

We in our exile have sent on ahead of us our advocate who, as mother of our Judge and mother of mercy, will humbly and effectively look after everything that concerns our salvation. Today earth has sent a priceless gift up to heaven, so that by giving and receiving within the blessed bond of friendship, the human is wedded to the divine, earth to heaven, the depths to the heights. ... Blessed indeed is Mary, blessed in many ways, both in receiving the Savior, and in being received by the Savior.

St. Bernard of Clairvaux

Mary must always have been a merciful person — long before the Crucifixion, before the public ministry of Christ, before his birth, before conceiving him in her womb, even before becoming betrothed to Joseph. I can picture Mary as a small child, sharing all she had, trying to console her playmates when they got hurt, searching for ways to fulfill the needs of others. As she grew older, her works of mercy would have increased. Of all the young girls in Nazareth, she was the most merciful. As a consecrated virgin, then, she was — and still is — the Virgin Most Merciful.

> *The works of mercy* are charitable actions by which we come to the aid of our neighbor in his spiritual and bodily necessities. Instructing, advising, consoling, comforting are spiritual works of mercy, as are forgiving and bearing wrongs patiently. The corporal works of mercy consist especially in feeding the hungry, sheltering the homeless, clothing the naked, visiting the sick and imprisoned, and burying the dead. Among all these, giving alms to the poor is one of the chief witnesses to fraternal charity: it is also a work of justice pleasing to God. (CCC 2447)

We know from the Archangel Gabriel that Mary was "full of grace," meaning that she was perfectly free from the stain of original sin. Because of this, she was perfectly free to love God and neighbor, as we are all called to do. Though we have only a few details from Scripture about her acts of mercy, we know that Mary perfectly emanated God's mercy to others.

We find one of the most telling examples of Mary's mercifulness at the Annunciation. Artists throughout the centuries have attempted to capture this monumental moment in the history of the world in their paintings. My favorite is by seventeenth-century artist Philippe de Champaigne, simply titled *The Annunciation.*[1] Like many other paintings of the Annunciation, it shows Mary at prayer as the archangel enters her chamber. This one, however, shows Gabriel holding a stalk of lilies (symbolizing Mary's purity as an avowed virgin) and two smaller angels hovering above the scene as the Holy Spirit waits to descend upon her. The expression on Mary's face speaks of both surprise and knowing — surprise at the approach and request of Gabriel and knowing that she must do whatever God desires. Gabriel asks her to be the mother of God, and she immediately agrees. In this moment Mary's mercy pours forth. She chooses to sacrifice the life she thought she would have as a solitary virgin dedicated to prayer and praising God so that mankind could be saved from sin and damnation. She consents to becoming the mother of the Merciful Savior even though it will mean great hardship and suffering. In that moment, Mary becomes the most powerful instrument of God's mercy.

Even now, she continues to mediate his mercy in a singular way, constantly giving of herself and caring for us so that we may spend eternity with God. For this reason, we call her Virgin Most Merciful.

REFLECTION

To be merciful means to be kind, compassionate, and forgiving toward others, just as God is toward us. When we show mercy to others, we reflect God's divine mercy and open a path for their deeper conversion, and our own. Mary helps us perform works of mercy, when we imitate her in giving of our time, energy, and even resources.

PRAYER

Mary, I yearn to have a heart as pure and merciful as yours, despite my human limitations. Help me to be an instrument of God's mercy in today's merciless world. Amen.

Virgin Most Faithful

After a long time, the master of those servants came back and settled accounts with them. The one who had received five talents came forward bringing the additional five. He said, "Master, you gave me five talents. See, I have made five more." His master said to him, "Well done, my good and faithful servant. Since you were faithful in small matters, I will give you great responsibilities. Come, share your master's joy."

Matthew 25:19–21 (NABRE)

At my father's funeral, the words from the parable of the talents in Matthew's Gospel came to my mind. Dad had spent his life trying to be faithful to God despite heartbreaks, hardships, and drawbacks. Still, he managed as best he could, and it was time for him to return to his Master. I prayed that, upon his death, Dad had heard the heavenly Father's voice say, "Well done, my good and faithful servant." That moment has stuck with me, and I have applied that Scripture passage to my own life, trying hard to remain faithful to God despite my own weaknesses and difficulties. I constantly remind myself that, when I die, I want to hear the heavenly Father's voice say those words to me. I desire to serve him always and in everything I do, even though I fall short at times.

Mary is the absolute example of faithfulness in heartbreaks, hardships, and drawbacks. Through the uncertainty and danger of becoming the mother of God, the flight to Egypt, a life of poverty, following Jesus through his public ministry, and then remaining at his side during his passion, crucifixion, and burial, she remained faithful. For her entire life, her every thought, word, and action were completely devoted to God. She never wavered in that fidelity. Mary was and is the Virgin Most Faithful.

In his providence, God gave the Blessed Mother a most faithful spouse. Saint Joseph was chaste, totally devoted to God, and always in control of his passions and sexuality. Fr. Donald Calloway, MIC, explained this in his book *Consecration to St. Joseph*:

> Saint Joseph and Mary lived in what is often called a "Josephite marriage." They were truly husband and wife, but they never engaged in sexual relations. Their vocation was to be united in heart, mind, and soul, but never in body. They were both consecrated to God and sacrificed a natural good for a greater good: the salvation of souls.[1]

Saint Joseph also trusted in God without wavering. Even though his senses told him otherwise, Saint Joseph trusted in the divinity of the tiny child in his care. He remained faithful to Jesus even in the most trying times and never hesitated in his role as guardian of Our Lord and his mother. He remained faithful to them throughout his life and even after his death. This is why he was the perfect spouse for Mary. As the Virgin Most Faithful, she needed a spouse who would not hinder her faithfulness to God. Her entire life was focused on one thing only: to constantly serve God in all that she said, did, thought, or experienced. No other human being was, is, or will be as capable of such profound faithfulness.

REFLECTION

Mary and Joseph were faithful to each other and to God, and they are also faithful to us. All that they did and endured was for the sake of our salvation. They continue to remain faithful to us, interceding for us in all our needs, sharing in our joys, and comforting us in our sorrows.

PRAYER

O Mary, O Saint Joseph, you are most faithful to God. Help me to trust that you are also always faithful to me. Show me how to be truly faithful to God and his will for my life. Amen.

MIRROR OF JUSTICE

Near indeed is his salvation for those who fear him;
glory will dwell in our land.
Love and truth will meet;
justice and peace will kiss.
Truth will spring from the earth;
justice will look down from heaven.
Yes, the Lord will grant his bounty;
our land will yield its produce.
Justice will march before him
and make a way for his footsteps.

Psalm 85:10–14 (NABRE)

We so often hear people crying out for justice in the media and movies. In courtrooms — real and fictitious — lawyers fight for justice for their clients. The United States calls one of the three branches of government the judicial branch, and the administration of its principles is referred to as the justice system. There are both secular and religious groups whose sole mission is social justice. My own diocese, the Archdiocese of Milwaukee, for example, has an Office of Social Justice whose mission is the "defense of human dignity, human rights, and the pursuit of justice and peace."[1] But what is justice? More specifically, what is justice in the realm of God? That, in the end, is the only justice that matters.

The *Catechism*'s glossary defines justice as a moral virtue "which consists in the constant and firm will to give their due to God and to neighbor." It delineates four types of justice: *original justice*, or the state of holiness in which God created our first parents (Adam and Eve); *commutative justice*, or the obligation to respect the rights of others; *legal justice*, or what the citizen owes to the community; and *distributive justice*, or what the community owes its citizens. Jesus summarized these forms of justice when he gave the first and second greatest commandments to the inquisitive Pharisees. "'You shall love the Lord your God with all your heart, and with all your soul, and with all your mind.' This is the greatest and first commandment. And a second is like it: 'You shall love your neighbor as yourself.' On these two commandments hang all the law and the prophets" (Mt 22:37–40).

One of the invocations in the Litany of the Sacred Heart is "Heart of Jesus, source of justice and love," and in the Litany of the Holy Name of Jesus he is called, "Jesus, dawn of justice." We know that the Almighty is a God of love, for "whoever does not love does not know God, for God is love" (1 Jn 4:8). But he is also a God of justice. The Prophet Isaiah tells us, "For the Lord is a God of justice; /blessed are all those who wait for him" (Is 30:18). We could say, then, that Our Lord is not only a just God, but he is Justice itself. And since Jesus was born of Mary, carrying her genes and likeness, it is fitting to call her the Mirror of Justice. For she not only resembles him physically, but also in all her characteristics. If Our Lord is just, then our Blessed Mother is just, since she cannot do anything that is not in accord with her son.

REFLECTION

To be just means to act according to principles of moral rightness and decency. A just person exercises righteousness in all that he thinks, says, and does. God is just, and he wills that we, too, should be just in all things in imitation of him.

PRAYER

Mary, Mirror of Justice, help me to mirror Our Lord's justice in my own life. It can be so difficult! Pray for me and accompany me as I try to live up to the example you have set for me. Amen.

Seat of Wisdom

Wisdom teaches her children
and gives help to those who seek her.
Whoever loves her loves life,
and those who seek her from early
morning are filled with joy.
Whoever holds her fast inherits glory,
and the Lord blesses the place she enters.
Those who serve her minister to the Holy One;
the Lord loves those who love her.

Sirach 4:11–14

In the small village of Houghton St. Giles in Norfolk, England, rests a fourteenth-century chapel where the statue of Our Lady of Walsingham is enshrined. It is called the Slipper Chapel, presumably because pilgrims would stop there and remove their shoes before walking the final mile to the King's Lynn shrine in Walsingham, home of a replica of the Holy House of Loreto dating back to the eleventh century.[1] Both shrines are filled with historical significance, but the aspect that most intrigues me is the statue of Our Lady of Walsingham in the Slipper Chapel.

The statue shows Mary seated on a throne, wearing a Saxon crown symbolizing her ancient queenship, and holding a three-fold lily scepter, symbolizing her virginity and sovereignty. The poles on either side of the backrest contain seven golden rings for the seven sacraments, and the spaces between stand for the Church. The arch on the backrest is formed and engraved in the shape of a rainbow, denoting the covenant God made with his people. The throne rests on a toadstone, an East Anglian symbol of evil. The Christ Child is seated on Mary's lap, holding the Gospels and extending his arm in a dual gesture of blessing and protection of his mother. Mary holds the child securely, with one hand pointing toward him in keeping with her mission of leading the world to him.[2]

In his First Letter to the Corinthians, Saint Paul refers to Jesus as "the wisdom of God": "For Jews demand signs and Greeks desire wisdom, but we proclaim Christ crucified, a stumbling block to Jews and foolishness to Gentiles, but to those who are the called, both Jews and Greeks, Christ the power of God and the wisdom of God" (1:22–24).

Since God is utterly simple, his nature is not distinct from his attributes (such as his goodness, mercy, justice, or wisdom) as ours are (nor are these attributes distinct from one another in him as they are in us). God is not simply wise; he is Wisdom itself. And who does Mary, as depicted in images like Our Lady of Walsingham, hold in her lap? Jesus. And who is Jesus? He is God, who is Wisdom. And since Mary's lap forms a seat for our little Lord, then she truly is the Seat of Wisdom.

We could carry this line of thought further yet. Because she did not suffer the consequences of original sin, Mary is perfect, which means her reasoning is perfect, making her wise above all other human beings. She is directly related to Jesus and so shares in his human traits, and he in hers. Remember that Our

Lord lived at home with Mary until he was thirty years old, and, in that time, he was able to increase her knowledge and wisdom. Just as the Wisdom Books of the Bible (Job, Psalms, Proverbs, Ecclesiastes, Song of Songs, Wisdom, and Sirach) refer to Our Lord as Wisdom, we could say that those passages also refer to our Blessed Mother Mary — the Seat of Wisdom.

REFLECTION

Of all human beings, Mary knows Our Lord best. When Jesus was young, she taught him, but when Jesus was older, he taught her. Mary was wise on her own, but Our Lord increased her wisdom throughout the years. We go to Mary to seek her wisdom and, in turn, she leads us to Wisdom himself.

PRAYER

O Mary, Seat of Wisdom, intercede for me before your son. Ask him to grant me a share in his wisdom so that I can come to know him more deeply and lead others to him as you do. Amen.

Cause of Our Joy

The pleasant companionship of all the blessed in heaven will be a companionship replete with delight. For each one will possess all good things together with the blessed, because they will love one another as themselves, and therefore will rejoice in the happiness of others' goods as well as their own. Consequently, the joy and gladness of one will be as great as the joy of all.

St. Thomas Aquinas

Mary was a real human woman who experienced the same emotions and struggles that all women face. I love to consider various scenes in Mary's life and what they would have been like for her. In particular, at Pentecost, we see Mary as a woman of profound joy. Imagine her elation at the descent of the Holy Spirit and the sudden courage and enthusiasm of the apostles as they shed their cowardly demeanor and took to the streets to proclaim Jesus Christ to the crowds, baptizing three thousand in a single day. These men were her son's best friends, and she loved them because he loved them. Just weeks before, they had denied and abandoned him, but now they were filled with zeal to carry out his directive and build his Church on earth. All that Jesus had lived, worked, and suffered for was coming to fruition through these men. Mary must have been filled with utter pride and joy.

Mary had always followed God's commandments and delighted in serving him entirely. She remained ever joyful, wrapped in the cloak of God's love. Even in the darkest moments, she might not have been happy, but she would have had boundless joy in God's perfect and providential plan. She knew that God is a loving Father who can have no part in cruelty. This was her motivation in saying yes to becoming the mother of Our Lord. She must have sensed that it would not be easy, but she rejoiced in being God's instrument for the salvation of all humankind. She rejoiced at becoming Christ's mother and, at that same time, our mother since we are members of the Body of Christ, the Church. Just as she found immense joy in seeing the apostles courageously assume Our Lord's mission, she finds immense joy is seeing us do the same. She wants each of us to share in the magnificence of heaven, to be part of the blessed companionship and jubilation of all who dwell there in God's presence. Had it not been for Mary's yes to Gabriel at the Annunciation, the Savior would not have been born, and the gates of heaven would not have been opened to us. By agreeing to God's request, she became the Cause of Our Joy.

REFLECTION

The very thought of Mary's yes to God should fill us with unmitigated joy. Her yes not only opened the gates of heaven, but also gave us the Eucharist so that we can be completely united with Jesus.

PRAYER

O Mary, Cause of Our Joy, show me how to be as joyful as you in even the most dire circumstances. You found your joy in God alone; help me to do the same. Amen.

Spiritual Vessel

O blessed and ever-blessed Virgin, by whose blessing not only is every creature blessed by its Creator, but the Creator is blessed by the creature!

St. Anselm of Canterbury

We won't know until we get to heaven exactly what the Blessed Mother looks like. Even in her many apparitions, her appearance varies. Yet we can know her character with certainty. Mary was a woman of extraordinary strength, filled with joy, love, and humility. Her life was as extraordinary as her spiritual depth, and she accepted everything that happened to her with grace, prudence, and devotion. She was a woman of great contemplation, as we know from Saint Luke's account of the Nativity: "But Mary treasured all these words and pondered them in her heart" (Lk 2:19). Mary knew the greatest secret of all time — the Incarnation — and yet she serenely held it in her heart until God chose to reveal it in his way and in his time. She bore within herself the most profound spiritual treasures of God, including the God-Man himself. This is why she is referred to as a spiritual vessel.

I often wonder what it would have been like to be present at the Nativity — as a simple shepherd, perhaps, who had heard the tidings of great joy proclaimed by the angels. Although Mary could have drawn attention to her own importance, she did not. She was, of course, blessed among women and worthy of distinction. I can imagine her being very soft-spoken and measured in her words and actions, remaining centered upon the Child in the manger. Filled to overflowing with love for God, she was concerned only with allowing the Savior to be recognized and worshiped. The graces and mysteries she held within were not to be flaunted, but to be kept and nurtured.

There is a passage in Paul's Second Letter to the Corinthians that perfectly sums up what I perceive to be Mary's attitude, not just at the Nativity, but always:

> For we do not preach ourselves but Jesus Christ as Lord, and ourselves as your slaves for the sake of Jesus. For God who said, "Let light shine out of darkness," has shone in our hearts to bring to light the knowledge of the glory of God on the face of [Jesus] Christ. But we hold this treasure in earthen vessels, that the surpassing power may be of God and not from us. (4:5–7, NABRE)

Mary did not preach about herself, even though she had a reason to do so. She preached only Our Lord, making herself a slave to the will of God. At the Nativity, Mary allowed the Light to shine in the darkness, to bring peace, joy, and salvation to all mankind. This Light shown forth from her wherever she went and even when she was not near Jesus. She was not the source of the surpassing power of God, but a vessel from which it radiated. And all these things, she pondered in her heart — a true Spiritual Vessel.

REFLECTION

It is normal to want to be honored for who we are and what we do. We want to feel worthy and capable. But we often forget that everything we are and do comes from God and belongs to him. Like Mary, we need to take time to ponder these things in our hearts so that we can become genuinely spiritual beings, radiating God's surpassing power always.

PRAYER

Mary, Spiritual Vessel, please pray for me to have the gift of contemplation as you did. Guard me from becoming pompous and self-centered. Like you, I want to be able to ponder the mystery and glory of God. Amen.

Vessel of Honor

In a large house there are utensils not only of gold and silver but also of wood and clay, some for special use, some for ordinary. All who cleanse themselves of the things I have mentioned will become special utensils, dedicated and useful to the owner of the house, ready for every good work.

2 Timothy 2:20–21

In daily living, the word *vessel* can mean different things. It can refer to a ship, barge, or any kind of craft that travels on water and holds either passengers, cargo, or both. It also can be a basin, pitcher, pot, bucket, or anything else that holds something. In our Catholic Faith, we have sacred vessels used during Holy Mass — the chalice, paten, ciborium — all of which hold the Body and Blood of Jesus Christ. Other sacred vessels include the aspergillum, which holds holy water, used by the priest during special blessings; the thurible, which holds burning incense; the boat, which holds the incense to be burned; and the monstrance, which holds a large consecrated Host during Eucharistic adoration. In general, vessels hold something important or useful. The sacred vessels of holy Mass hold Something (or Someone) Divine.

Mary, too, is a sacred vessel, as she bore Our Lord, the Second Person of the Holy Trinity. As we know from the teachings of the Catholic Church, the Trinity is "the mystery of one God in three Persons: Father, Son, and Holy Spirit" (CCC Glossary). As such, the Persons of the Trinity cannot be separated, and so we can say that Mary held within herself Father, Son, and Holy Spirit. During her pregnancy, she contained Something Divine, just like the vessels at Mass. No other human being has been or will be given this same honor!

Have you ever noticed the careful protocol with which the sacred vessels are handled and used at Mass? The priest, deacon, altar servers, and extraordinary ministers of the holy Eucharist treat the vessels with the utmost reverence. They are picked up and put down ever so gently, cleaned only with the prescribed cloths and in an exact order, and stored in a place of respect and safety. They indeed are vessels of honor, sanctified and made useful to the Master and prepared for a specific purpose.

Can we not say the same of our Blessed Mother? She was sanctified by Christ, preserved from the stain of original sin, and helpful to the Master for one purpose alone: to be the mother of his only-begotten Son. Because of her yes to become the mother of God, she became our mother as well, spiritually.

REFLECTION

As the vessel who bore Christ, Mary deserves our utmost reverence. We can honor her, the perfect Vessel of Honor, in the ways we pray to, talk about, study, and imitate her in our daily lives.

PRAYER

Mary, Vessel of Honor and my mother, I want to honor you as I should. Help me to remain pure, dignified, and helpful to the Master as you were. Amen.

Singular Vessel of Devotion

Happy are those whose way is blameless,
who walk in the law of the Lord.
Happy are those who keep his decrees,
who seek him with their whole heart,
who also do no wrong,
but walk in his ways.

Psalm 119:1–3

St. Francis de Sales tells us that true devotion is love of God in the highest form. In his book *An Introduction to the Devout Life*, he wrote the following:

> Indeed it is itself a true love of him in the highest form, for whereas divine love enlightening our soul is called Grace, and makes us pleasing in his sight; so giving us power to do good, it is called Charity; and when it reaches that point of perfection wherein it not only causes us to do good, but

> to do it earnestly, frequently, and readily, then it is called Devotion.

Mary's devotion was true love of God in the highest form. Clearly, divine love had enlightened her soul, because the Archangel Gabriel addressed her as "full of grace." As the only creature to ever be exempt from the effects of original sin, she was pleasing in God's sight. If she were not, God would not have chosen her to be the mother of his Son. Mary had the gift of perfect charity, giving all of herself to God's will for our sakes. There was no hesitation in her love for and obedience to God, even though it may have seemed so when she asked Gabriel how it was possible that she could conceive when she was a virgin (and, we believe, had made a private vow to remain so). Her question was not one of doubt in God's providence, but concern to honor his request fully and promptly.

No one could ever be as devoted to God as Mary was, and for this reason we call her devotion "singular." When we speak of singularity, we are referring to something that is unique and of immeasurable value. Not only was the magnitude of her devotion unparalleled, but she was — and is — unparalleled in her very being! God chose Mary above all women of all time to be mother of our Savior and his helpmate in his plan of salvation. There is and can be only one Mother of God, and to merit such a prominent position, she had to be perfect in all ways. There is no one as perfect, obedient, loving, or devoted as Mary.

Her devotion stems from her pure and selfless heart that seeks only to please God. This devotion wells up within her and flows outward, giving glory to God. Her heart is a fount of true devotion to God and inexhaustible love for us. Such devotion cannot be found in any other human being, and so we aptly call Mary the Singular Vessel of Devotion.

REFLECTION

Devotion is the sum of fervor, piety, praise, and worship. We are called to be devoted to God as Mary was, to obey him as she did, and to love him in the way that she did. It is a high calling, but one for which God will grant us the necessary graces.

PRAYER

Mary, Singular Vessel of Devotion, and my gentle mother, pray for me, that my devotion to God will be pure and persistent, as yours is. Amen.

Mystical Rose

I am a rose of Sharon,
a lily of the valleys.
As a lily among brambles,
so is my love among maidens.

Song of Songs 2:1–2

The rose has been a celebrated flower throughout the centuries and across many cultures. Think of the plentitude of Valentine's Day advertisements that urge us to present our beloved with a dozen red roses. One need only do a quick internet search to find a list of rose festivals held throughout the United States and around the world. Prestigious estates, municipalities, botanical gardens, and gardening societies commonly have elaborate rose gardens. Even the library of my small hometown has a collection of antique rose bowls, gifted by the heiress of a wealthy Irish immigrant industrialist.

In her book *A Garden Catechism*, master gardener and Catholic author Margaret Rose Realy, Obl. OSB, wrote, "The rose has been part of our heritage for centuries, being initially portrayed in the Old Testament." She tells of an ancient legend about the Blessed Virgin Mary. The rose had no thorns before the Fall of Man, and so Mary is referred to as the "rose without thorns" because she was untouched by original sin. This is why sacred art so often depicts her with roses, especially in scenes of the Immaculate Conception, Assumption, and Coronation.[1]

Given the value and symbolism of roses, it is easy to see why Our Lady would be referred to as a rose. But why a *mystical* rose? When we consider an earthly garden, it does not make sense. When we consider God's spiritual garden, however — a place of spiritual tranquility, peace, renewal, and joy — we can see how Mary would be the Mystical Rose in God's mystical garden, or paradise. St. John Henry Newman described it this way: "Mary is the most beautiful flower that ever was seen in the spiritual world. It is by the power of God's grace that from this barren and desolate earth there have ever sprung up at all flowers of holiness and glory. And Mary is the queen of them."[2] Furthermore, he explained, she is a mystical rose because she was taken up to heaven, body and soul.

Like a carefully cultivated garden rose, Mary is both delicate and strong, captivating and delightful. She is queen among the blossoms, beautiful beyond compare, perfect in every way, and glorious to behold. She was created this way to be worthy of being the Mother of God. The perfectly created being gave birth to the perfect Creator. This is a mystery that human understanding cannot fathom but must only accept. Mary is the fairest of the fair, the prize bloom of the Master Gardener, the Mystical Rose.

REFLECTION

In the ancient legend, Mary is described as "the rose without thorns" because she was untouched by original sin. Therefore, she is the model for all human beings. Of course, we are touched by original sin, but we still can strive each day to resemble the Mystical Rose as much as possible.

PRAYER

Mary, Mystical Rose, pray for me. In my human thinking, I don't always know how to appreciate your beauty and perfection. Help me to slow down and take in all the facets of your grace and elegance so that I can learn to love you as you deserve. Amen.

TOWER OF DAVID

Your neck is like the tower of David,
built in courses;
on it hang a thousand bucklers,
all of them shields of warriors.

Song of Songs 4:4

One of Gideon's sons, Abimelech, was born of a concubine from Shechem. After Gideon's death, Abimelech became judge of Israel and sought to rule over Shechem as well. His methodology, unfortunately, was not forthright. Rather than earning his place of rule justly, he chose to gain the title by eliminating his opposition. Abimelech's heart was filled with greed and envy, and he became a tyrannical and cruel ruler, causing a conspiracy to arise against him. A civil war broke out, leading to a battle in the town of Thebez. With Abimelech approaching, all the men and women and lords of the city fled to a high tower and shut themselves up in it for protection. Abimelech saw his opportunity and trapped the city leaders in the tower with the intent to burn it down with everyone in it. Just then one of the women in the tower threw down a millstone and crushed Abimelech's head (see Jgs 9).

The details of this story are less important for our purposes than one single fact: The people fled to a tower for protection against evil. The Blessed Mother is a spiritual tower to whom we flee for protection against evil. What is more, she is referred to as the Tower of David and not just any tower. The Tower of David, also known as the Jerusalem Citadel, guards the holy city of Jerusalem, just as Mary guards God's holy city — the People of God. From the top of the Tower of David, one has a 360-degree view of both the Old City and the more modern areas of Jerusalem. So, too, Mary has a 360-degree view of God's people, both old and new, a right she is given because of her closeness to the Trinity. The Tower of David is one of Israel's most cherished historical sites. In an even broader spiritual sense, Mary is one of salvation history's most cherished figures.[1]

Mary, the Tower of David, has been charged with the task of fighting Satan on our behalf. In the Garden of Eden, God told the serpent, "I will put enmity between you and the woman and between your offspring and hers" (Gn 3:15). St. Louis de Montfort wrote: "It is between Mary, his worthy mother, and the devil — between the children and the servants of the Blessed Virgin, and the children and tools of Lucifer. The most terrible of all the enemies which God has set up against the devil is his holy mother Mary."[2] This enemy of the devil is our own Mother Mary, the Tower of David, who beckons to us to flee to her for safety.

REFLECTION

We are faced with evil every day, all day long and through the night. Satan is always chomping at the bit, tempting us to turn away from God. He wants everyone to be as miserable as he is. This is why it is critical to cling to Mary, to take refuge in the Tower of David the second we feel the pull of temptation. Within her motherly arms and behind her shield of victory, we are assured of her protection.

PRAYER

Mary, help me to see you as the Tower of David, my place of safety and protection against evil. Let me never forget that you are constantly there, armed and ready to fight the evil one on my behalf. Amen.

Tower of Ivory

It is true: therefore, she is called the Tower of Ivory, to suggest to us, by the brightness, purity, and exquisiteness of that material, how transcendent is the loveliness and the gentleness of the Mother of God.

St. John Henry Newman[1]

Since biblical times, ivory has been a precious and coveted material. We read about it in the Second Book of Chronicles when the ships of Tarshish came bringing gold, silver, ivory, apes, and peacocks (see 9:21); in Kings when Ahab built a house of ivory (1 Kgs 22:39); in Ezekiel when ivory was used as payment along with ebony (Ez 27:15); and John describes an ivory throne in Revelation (Rv 20:11). Ivory was a symbol of royalty, honor, and prestige. In more modern times, we hear about the scourge of poachers killing African elephants for their ivory tusks. In 1989, the Convention on International Trade in Endangered Species of Wild Fauna and Flora (CITES) passed a law against poaching elephants to curb the estimated 100,000 elephants being killed annually. Sadly, the law has not ended the practice.[2]

While it may have been difficult at first to imagine Mary as the Tower of David, perhaps it is easier to imagine her as the Tower of Ivory. Ivory is pure, white (as in spotless), flawless, and strong. Thrones, buildings, art, and other items made of ivory withstand the test of time and still maintain their beauty. Ivory is precious because of its expense and rarity. Think now about our Blessed Mother. Is she not also pure, spotless, flawless, and strong? Most certainly she is beautiful to behold, as we have heard from the seers of Marian apparitions throughout the centuries. Yes, we can easily compare Mary to the most valuable ivory ever created.

But why do we call her a tower of ivory? Why not a vessel of some kind, or a fine piece of jewelry? Because Mary is indeed a tower above all other creatures. As a tower rises high above the neighboring structures, Mary rises high above all other beings in her holiness and honor. She rose above all other women to become Mother of the Redeemer. She rose above the apostles in her faithfulness to Jesus during his mission, passion, and crucifixion. The apostles all fled when Our Lord was in his greatest need; Mary did not. She rises above all the warriors in God's kingdom fighting the evil one. Mary is a tower, a graceful, lovely, strong, venerable, pure, faithful, and true tower. She is the Tower of Ivory.

REFLECTION

Like ivory, Mary is both strong and spotless. Original sin has left us with shortcomings and weaknesses that hold us back, making us look more like dilapidated towers made of old wood. We can, however, remain close to Mary, allowing her beauty and grace to reflect upon us. By her side, we will be encouraged to strive for the heights of love and devotion to God.

PRAYER

Mary, I wish I could behold your beauty, purity, and grace. I would like to see you as God's beloved Tower of Ivory and to remain safely beside you always. Pray for me, please, that I may increasingly resemble you throughout my life. Amen.

House of Gold

And I will put this third into the fire,
refine them as one refines silver,
and test them as gold is tested.
They will call on my name,
and I will answer them.
I will say, "They are my people;"
and they will say, "The Lord is our God."

Zechariah 13:9

When Solomon built the Temple, he wanted it to be a place that truly gave glory to God and that was a reminder to the people of God's majesty and might. He brought in tradesmen from foreign countries, experts at their craft, to create the ornate and costly trappings of God's house. In the First Book of Kings, we read about the materials and the great care with which they were used:

> So Solomon made all the vessels that were in the house of the Lord: the golden altar, the golden table for the

> bread of the Presence, the lampstands of pure gold, five on the south side and five on the north, in front of the inner sanctuary; the flowers, the lamps, and the tongs, of gold; the cups, snuffers, basins, dishes for incense, and firepans, of pure gold, the sockets for the doors of the innermost part of the house, the most holy place, and for the doors of the nave of the temple, of gold. (7:48–50)

Solomon chose to adorn the Temple in gold because gold is a symbol of royalty, prosperity, and dignity. For God, Solomon wanted only the absolute best. We have no images of Solomon's Temple, but from the biblical descriptions, it must have been a work of magnificence and splendor.

Mary also is a work of magnificence and splendor. When searching for a worthy temple to house his Son, the heavenly Father chose only the absolute best — Mary. For nine months, this simple Jewish maiden would nurture the Second Person of the Trinity within her; she would be the Temple of the Lord, the house in which he lived from conception to birth. She was chosen because of her fine qualities, perfection, dignity, and value among all women. There was no other creature worthy of bearing the Son of God, the King of Kings, who deserves a dwelling fit for a king. He deserves a House of Gold.

It is overwhelming to think that a woman could conceive and bear the Almighty, All-Powerful, All-Knowing, All-Present King of the Universe. It is far easier to comprehend the mothers of saints, who conceive, bear, give birth to, and raise holy sons and daughters who one day reach the throne of sanctity. But to house God himself is unfathomable in terms of the honor and responsibility. It is not that I doubt the Incarnation, but rather that I am stunned by God's goodness and mercy in sending his only-begotten Son to take human form so that he could redeem the world! And so, this Mighty King could have only the finest quarters: a House of Gold.

REFLECTION

Like Mary, we also should strive to be houses of gold. We should always be conscious of the fact that we are temples of the Holy Spirit. God wants to dwell within us, and we must do our best to be a worthy dwelling for the Triune God, to behave always with purity and dignity, allowing all that we are and do to give glory to God.

PRAYER

Mary, House of Gold, please help me to become a house of gold, too. Intercede for me in my brokenness that I may be purified in my thoughts and deeds, so that I may give glory to God every minute of my life. Amen.

Ark of the Covenant

The Blessed Virgin, by becoming the mother of God, received a kind of infinite dignity because God is infinite; this dignity therefore is such a reality that a better one is not possible, just as nothing can be better than God.

St. Thomas Aquinas

God gave Moses two stone tablets that had the Ten Commandments etched on them. The Commandments were God's Word, and the hand that etched them was God's. They were a symbol of God's covenant with his people. To the Israelites, those stones were sacred, requiring veneration and care. They knew that they must not be left lying out in the open, lest the elements wear away the stone or some other mishap damage them. They needed to be contained in a sturdy receptacle that would keep them safe and at the same time be transportable to accompany the Israelites on their journey.

For this purpose, Moses commissioned the craftsman Bezalel to build an ark, similar in principle to the ark of Noah, which kept precious cargo safe during the Great Flood. The ark was made of acacia wood overlaid with pure gold inside and outside and with a molding of gold around it. Bezalel cast four gold rings and attached two on each side so that acacia-wood poles could be run through them, allowing the ark to be carried reverently. He also made a pure gold mercy seat with a golden cherub on each end. The cherubim were magnificent, with wings that spread wide over the mercy seat (see Ex 37:1–9). The ark was made in exact measurements prescribed by Moses and formed to perfectly fit the Ten Commandments. The ark was perfect, or as perfect as any human hand could make it. Because of its holy contents, the ark became known as the Ark of the Covenant.

Mary also was formed with precision and of precious materials. She carried Our Lord in her womb, not the symbol of the Old Covenant of God with his people, but instead the New Covenant himself. She has continued her role throughout time, spiritually carrying the Holy One from country to country, church to church, home to home, and heart to heart. She will forever proceed on her mission, carrying Christ to all in all places.

In the Old Testament, the Holy of Holies contained a golden tabernacle in which the Ark of the Covenant resided when the Israelites were encamped. The tabernacles in our churches are the descendants of the Old Testament tabernacle, and they hold something precious: Jesus in the Eucharist, truly present in his Body, Blood, Soul, and Divinity. Because Mary cannot be separated from her son, she is there, too, in the tabernacle, the holy Ark of the Covenant.

REFLECTION

The scribes and Pharisees accused Jesus of leading others into disobeying the law of the prophets — that is, the teachings of

Moses based on the Ten Commandments. He told them, "Do not think that I have come to abolish the law or the prophets; I have come not to abolish but to fulfill" (Mt 5:17). We could say that this was Mary's purpose as well. She brought forth the Savior who would, with his own Body and Blood, establish the New Covenant.

PRAYER

O Mary, become for me the Ark of the Covenant. Carry your son to me, rest him deeply in my heart, and accompany me on every step of my journey to heaven. Help me to fervently believe in and worthily receive the holy Eucharist. Amen.

Gate of Heaven

It was through Mary that the salvation of the world was begun, and it is through Mary that it must be consummated.

St. Louis de Montfort

Gates have a dual purpose. They can give entrance or they can block entrance. Stop and think for a minute about all the gates that you see and pass through on an average day. There probably are a lot! There are many gates that appear in Scripture, but they differ from the gates with which we are familiar today. In biblical times, gates usually symbolized the structure that they protected. Taking "possession" of the enemy's gate meant that they had been conquered and captured. For example, the Israelites took possession of the gates of their enemies, signifying their dominance over them. The gates of Jerusalem were sacred because they protected the holy city and the Temple within its walls.

Jesus taught about another kind of gate: the gate of the sheepfold. He told his disciples: "Very truly, I tell you, anyone who does not enter the sheepfold by the gate but climbs in by another way is a thief and a bandit. The one who enters by the gate is the shepherd of the sheep. The gatekeeper opens the gate for him, and the sheep hear his voice" (Jn 10:1–3). Then Jesus told them that he himself is the gate to the sheepfold, comparing the sheepfold to his kingdom: "I am the gate. Whoever enters by me will be saved, and will come in and go out and find pasture" (Jn 10:9). Our Lord is absolutely direct here. Only those who follow his commandments will be welcome into heaven. The gate will be closed to those who do not.

In the Book of Genesis, we read about Jacob's fantastic dream, during which he saw a ladder reaching from earth to heaven. Angels were going up and down the ladder, when suddenly Jacob sensed that God was standing next to him. God said:

> I am the Lord, the God of Abraham your father and the God of Isaac; the land on which you lie I will give to you and to your offspring; your offspring shall be like the dust of the earth, and you shall spread abroad to the west and to the east and to the north and to the south; and all the families of the earth shall be blessed in you and in your offspring. Know that I am with you and will keep you wherever you go and will bring you back to this land; for I will not leave you until I have done what I have promised you. (28:13-15)

Jacob's ladder is identified as the gate of heaven and makes a fine symbol of Our Lady. It is almost as if God's words to Jacob apply to her as well. She is, as St. Louis de Montfort said in the quote above, the portal through which the salvation of the world was begun. The Redeemer was born of her womb; her body was the holy and ever-virgin gate through which he passed. When Mary became the mother of God, she became the mother of all peoples, and her spiritual offspring are as numerous as the dust of the earth, spread throughout the world over all time. Through Mary all families of the earth are blessed. Mary is the Gate of Heaven, and through her generous fiat, all her children are welcomed into the kingdom of God.

REFLECTION

By her consent to becoming the mother of Our Lord, Mary made it possible for us to enter heaven. She not only opened the gate of heaven, but she *is* the Gate of Heaven by her example of discipleship and intercession for us before her son. If we follow her closely, she will lead us to Jesus and guide us through the gate and into eternity.

PRAYER

Mary, thank you for making it possible for the gate of heaven to be opened to me. You have become for me — for all people — the Gate of Heaven. Please pray for me that I may merit the reward of heaven when I pass from this life. Amen.

Morning Star

As sailors are guided by a star to the port, so
Christians are guided to heaven by Mary.

St. Thomas Aquinas

The term *morning star* generally applies to the planet Venus, which appears in the east before sunrise, glowing with a steady, silvery light. But a morning star can also be any planet that rises at the crack of dawn and disappears by noon. In earlier times, the morning star helped those traveling by land and sea to navigate. Since it was steady and dependable, it could be counted on for accurate direction. These "stars" never appear far from the sun in the sky because they orbit the sun more closely than Earth does.[1]

Our Lady is also steady and dependable and never far from the Son. Wherever Jesus is, Mary is, and vice versa. Although not in the same way as the Holy Trinity, Our Lord and his mother can never be separated. They are bonded as mother and son both physically and spiritually, a relationship that is unique among all others. They are bound together in the plan of salvation — Jesus as Savior and Mary as his helpmate. Mary would have no light of her own were it not for her son; she continuously reflects his light.

Because of her place near her son and her role in his plan of salvation, Mary is our guide. She is there always, a beacon shining on our journey toward heaven. We can never go astray if we keep her in our sights. With her guiding us, we will never be lost. If we feel ourselves being tossed to and fro or lost in fog on the sea of life, we need only look to her. Unlike natural stars, Mary's brightness never fades; she is always visible in any kind of spiritual weather. According to St. John Henry Newman, "Morning Star" is the best of all of Mary's titles in the Litany of Loreto, for three reasons:

> Mary now has no part in this netherworld. No change, no violence from fire, water, earth, or air affects the stars above; and they show themselves, even bright and marvelous, in all regions of this globe, and to all the tribes of men. ... But Mary, like the stars, abides forever, as lustrous now as she was on the day of her Assumption; as pure and perfect, when her son comes in judgment, as she is now. Lastly, it is Mary's prerogative to be the Morning Star which heralds in the sun. She does not shine for herself, or of herself, but she is a reflection of her and our Redeemer, and she glorifies him. When she appears in the darkness, we know that he is close at hand.[2]

REFLECTION

So often when we are floundering, we stubbornly insist on figuring things out for ourselves. We may be completely lost but hesitant to seek direction. We want to power through even if it means wandering hopelessly and helplessly for an extended time. I know I do this far too much, and I imagine you tend to do it, too. How much easier things would be for us if only we could shed our stubbornness and remember to look to the Morning Star for guidance!

PRAYER

O Mary, Morning Star, do not let me be lost on the ocean of my life. Shine on me from your heavenly post, draw my attention to you, and be a reminder to me that, depending upon you, I will never be lost. Amen.

Health of the Sick

Only after the Last Judgment will Mary get any rest; from now until then, she is much too busy with her children.

St. John Vianney

Thérèse of Lisieux was only four and a half years old when her mother, Zélie Martin, died of breast cancer. After Zélie's death, Thérèse's older sister Pauline became her second mother, and the two became remarkably close. Five years later, Pauline entered the Carmelite cloister, leaving Thérèse once again without a mother. Even though her other sisters, Marie, Léonie, and Céline, tried their best to replace Pauline, Thérèse's heart was broken — so much so that she became gravely ill. The little girl was tucked into bed, delirious with fever and other mysterious symptoms, and it was feared that she would die.

One day, as Thérèse lay in bed, Marie prayed by her side, begging the Blessed Virgin Mary to cure the child. Kneeling, Marie turned to a statue of Mary that stood at the end of the bed. Léonie and Céline joined her in prayer, tears running down their cheeks. Reaching through the fog of her delirium, Thérèse prayed silently along with them. Then, a miraculous thing happened. Thérèse recounts:

> Suddenly the statue came to life, and Mary appeared utterly lovely, with a divine beauty I could not possibly describe. There was a wonderful sweetness and goodness about her face, and her expression was infinitely tender, but what went right to my heart was her smile. Then, all my pain was gone. Silently two big tears trickled down my cheeks, tears of complete and heavenly happiness. Our Lady had come to me![1]

This story of the Little Flower, as St. Thérèse called herself, is both touching and meaningful. The tenderness that Mary showed to her was not because she was a saint, but because Thérèse was her child, and her child needed comfort and healing. No doubt Thérèse was special to Mary, but so are we all. She loves each of us individually, tenderly, and devotedly. She will come to us when we are suffering, with her arms outstretched and smiling a divine smile. Compassion will flow from her mother heart, and she will heal us of our ailments — whether they be mental, emotional, or physical — according to God's will. There may be crosses and conditions that God wills for us for the sake of our salvation. Mary will never interfere with God's perfect plan. But she will accompany us in our suffering and give us the nurturing we need to sustain us.

Helping someone to endure sickness and suffering is also a form of healing, and Mary will extend that to us. Mary is Mother of the Divine Physician, Christ. She has learned from him to be a true healer and has been given the privilege to exercise that gift. Mary heals by interceding for us with her son, often in a miraculous way. Sometimes her healing comes slowly, almost imperceptibly, but it is healing just the same. There have been a multitude of healings through Mary's hands, including those that have occurred at Lourdes, Fátima, Champion, and through the Miraculous Medal. Some of these healings are immediate and obvious, others more obscure. But there is always some kind of healing. That is because Mary is the Health of the Sick.

REFLECTION

Sickness can be an overwhelming burden to bear. Even a brief bout of a cold or flu virus can leave us feeling weak and defeated. We are vulnerable when we are sick, and no one likes to feel that way. But it is in that vulnerability that we are most precious to Mother Mary, Health of the Sick.

PRAYER

Mary, Health of the Sick, I ask your healing for myself and my loved ones in all our infirmities. Reach out to us, scoop us up in your arms, and smile your heavenly smile of healing and comfort. Amen.

Refuge of Sinners

When she sees a sinner coming to implore mercy at her feet, she does not regard the sins with which he is laden, but the intention with which he comes.

St. Alphonsus de Liguori[1]

In biblical times, God commanded that there be cities of refuge that offered asylum to those who had committed involuntary manslaughter or other serious crimes. These people could flee to one of the cities of refuge and remain there, safe from punishment or revenge. The seeming criminal could remain safe in the city of refuge until a trial was held and he was proven innocent, or the current high priest passed away. Then the suspect could return home without consequence (see Jos 20:1–6). Biblical records show that there were six such cities in Jewish territory, three on either side of the Jordan River. There were more — as many as forty-eight — cities of refuge in surrounding areas. The ancient Greeks and Romans had cities of asylum as well, which served the same purpose. Christians carried on this custom, and in the Middle Ages the right of sanctuary allowed lawbreakers to take refuge in a church and remain there untouched.[2]

The concept of refuge is found close to one hundred times in Scripture.[3] The psalms sing the praises of God as the refuge of those in need of shelter and consolation. The prophets and writers of the Wisdom Books urge people to turn from their sinful ways and find refuge in God's commandments. Saint Paul writes extensively about finding refuge in Christ. And Our Lord himself beckons all to come to him and experience the refuge of his Sacred Heart: "Come to me, all you that are weary and are carrying heavy burdens, and I will give you rest. Take my yoke upon you, and learn from me, for I am gentle and humble in heart, and you will find rest for your souls. For my yoke is easy and my burden is light" (Mt 11:28–30).

Our Blessed Mother also has a gentle and humble heart, for her heart matches Christ's heart perfectly. Among Mary's primary responsibilities is that of extending her son's mercy to sinners. She is, after all, Mother of Mercy, having within herself a heart that aches for the conversion of sinners so that all her children will be welcomed into heaven at the end of time. Mary's heart is in essence a city of refuge like the ones in biblical times. But she offers refuge not just to those who have committed involuntary manslaughter, but also to those who have committed any type of sin, no matter how big or how small. What is more, she offers refuge to those who are tempted to sin and plagued by sinful weaknesses. She gathers us all in, shielding us from the demons that seek to tear us from the side of Christ. As the true Refuge of Sinners, Mary holds the keys to our conversion and transformation.

REFLECTION

The Church Fathers have taught that one small sin leads to other small sins and then larger and larger sins. Eventually, the unrepentant sinner turns from God completely, which is why we must be vigilant and resist even the smallest sin. In every weakness and temptation, we must run to Mary for her help and protection. She will offer us refuge from influences that could lead us to sin and give us strength to become better Christians.

PRAYER

O Mary, Refuge of Sinners, open your heart wide to me. Beckon to me in my weakness and shield me in my sinfulness so that I may never offend Our Lord again. Amen.

SOLACE OF MIGRANTS

For the common good, since it is intimately bound up with human nature, can never exist fully and completely unless the human person is taken into account at all times.

Pope St. John XXIII, *Pacem in Terris*

On June 20, 2020, Pope Francis added the invocation "Solace of Migrants" to the Litany of Loreto, stipulating that it should be added after "Refuge of Sinners." His purpose was to respond to the realities of our present-day world, in which people are forced from their homes because of poverty, war, and other hardships.[1]

Mary understands what it is like to be a migrant. The history of the Jewish people is a trail of migration from the earliest times. We could say that Adam and Eve migrated out of the Garden of Eden after the Fall. Noah and his family migrated to the ark during the Great Flood. Generations later, God commanded Abraham to leave his home and travel to the land he would designate. He told him:

> Go from your country and your kindred and your father's house to the land that I will show you. I will make of you a great nation, and I will bless you, and make your name great, so that you will be a blessing. I will bless those who bless you, and the one who curses you I will curse; and in you all the families of the earth shall be blessed. (Genesis 12:1–3)

The Israelites' wandering led them to Egypt where they were enslaved by Pharoah. They would not be free for four hundred years. From Egypt and under Moses' direction, they spent forty years crossing the desert until finally they entered the Promised Land. These were Mary's people, and she shared in their legacy of migration.

The Holy Family became migrants when they were forced to flee to Egypt to escape Herod's men. Herod sought to kill the Little King because he felt threatened by him and did not want to surrender his power. In a fit of rage, he ordered his henchmen to slaughter every first-born male child aged two and under in the city of Bethlehem. An angel warned Joseph in a dream of the impending danger, instructing him to promptly gather up his family and flee to Egypt where they remained for approximately three years, moving from place to place as fugitives.[2] We must consider the impact of the Holy Family's journey. They were suddenly uprooted from their home and sent to a foreign land where the language, food, people, and customs were vastly different. Additionally, they had no guaranteed source of income. Saint Joseph was a carpenter by trade, but would he find enough work to sustain them? These were unsettling circumstances, to say the least. Because of her own time as a migrant, Mary is especially equipped to offer solace to migrants.

REFLECTION

We all are migrants at times and in one way or another. Moving to a new area, starting a new job, changes in family structure, serious illness, or uncertainty of any kind are all forms of migration. While we may never experience the full extent of the suffering of being displaced from our homes, we can understand a little bit of the hopelessness and helplessness felt by migrants in any era. And we can take comfort in knowing that Mary, Solace of Migrants, has been there, too, and she is watching over those who are far from their homes.

PRAYER

Mary, Solace of Migrants, you endured extraordinary hardship during your flight to Egypt. You did it to save the life of your son, and for me, so that Jesus could eventually save the world through his suffering, death, and resurrection. Help me to be patient and strong in my times of migration, and to offer loving support to those who have been torn from their homes. Amen.

Comfort of the Afflicted

Come to me, all you that are weary and are carrying heavy burdens, and I will give you rest. Take my yoke upon you and learn from me; for I am gentle and humble in heart, and you will find rest for your souls. For my yoke is easy, and my burden is light.

Matthew 11:28–30

Saint Paul can teach us a lot about affliction. He suffered terribly throughout his life, facing spiritual battles, physical misery, imprisonment, poverty, and more. Yet in every affliction he gave thanks to God for the privilege of suffering like Our Lord and for the ability to comfort others in their troubles.

He wrote to the Corinthians:

> Blessed be the God and Father of our Lord Jesus Christ, the Father of mercies and God of all consolation, who consoles us in all our affliction, so that we may be able

> to console those who are in any affliction with the consolation with which we ourselves are consoled by God. For just as the sufferings of Christ are abundant for us, so also our consolation is abundant through Christ. (2 Corinthians 1:3–5)

It is a great gift to be able to console others because of our own experiences. Our suffering makes us able to sense the suffering of others with compassion and wisdom. We can console them because we understand how they feel and what they are going through. Each suffering is an opportunity, as Paul pointed out, to merit heaven and do good for others.

Mary suffered affliction as well. She and Saint Joseph lived in poverty, and so they had to work hard and make do with what little they had. We know this because they brought the prescribed offering of the less fortunate — two turtle doves or a pair of pigeons — when they presented Jesus in the Temple (see Lk 2:22–24). Mary suffered affliction when Jesus was lost for three days in Jerusalem. She and Joseph frantically searched for their son, and when they found him, they felt both pain and relief. Mary asked him: "Child, why have you treated us like this? Look, your father and I have been searching for you in great anxiety" (Lk 2:48). His answer left them even more hurt and puzzled. Mary suffered affliction during the Holy Family's flight to Egypt. They had to leave all that was familiar and secure and go forward into the unknown, encountering struggle after struggle (see Mt 2:13–15).

And, most difficult of all, Mary suffered grievous affliction during Our Lord's passion and death. We can gain an appreciation of the suffering in the traditional Lenten song, *Stabat Mater*. Each of the twenty verses reflects the agony her heart must have felt as she so helplessly watched the brutal torture and murder of her beloved son while bravely standing at the foot of the cross.[1]

There is no affliction like that of Mary on Good Friday.

REFLECTION

Because of the variety of afflictions that she withstood and her position as our mother, Mary is not only capable, but passionately driven to understand our suffering and tend to us in our affliction. At the least sign of distress, she rushes to our side, ready to console us. Her heart aches when ours does; she feels our burdens when we do. We are never alone in our affliction.

PRAYER

O Mary, sweet and sorrowful mother, you were troubled by affliction just as I am. You understand my suffering and have the intercessory power to alleviate it. Mary, Comfort of the Afflicted, gather me in your arms and enfold me in your tender care. Amen.

Help of Christians

Our Glorious Queen, since her assumption on high, has been the minister of numberless services to the elect people of God upon earth, and to his holy Church.

St. John Henry Newman, *The Mystical Rose*

In one of the most dramatic plays in the history of American football, Colorado's Kordell Stewart threw a pass to his teammate Michael Westbrook that sailed a full seventy-five yards and tipped right into Westbrook's hands. This daring play won the game for the Colorado Buffaloes against the Michigan Wolverines. It was a Hail Mary pass and would go down in the annals of football history as a remarkable athletic feat.[1]

A Hail Mary pass is a final, desperate effort to secure victory in a football game — usually with little chance of success. It is called a Hail Mary pass because of our Catholic tradition of praying the Hail Mary prayer for strength and help from the Blessed Mother in a tough situation. In my view, the Hail Mary pass is a beautiful, albeit unintentional, tribute to Mary. Even nonbelievers talk about Hail Mary passes and marvel at the athletic prowess involved. Whether they realize it or not, they are acknowledging the efficacy of the mother of God in assisting her children.

God has given Mary both the ability and responsibility to help us in our daily lives. While she most certainly is interested in the smallest of our needs and desires, she is mostly concerned with our salvation and protection against evil. One of the most famous examples of Mary's help during grave danger is the Battle of Lepanto on October 7, 1517. The Muslim Ottoman Empire threatened to take over all of Christendom. Pope Pius V gathered what Christian forces he could and sent them against the approaching Ottomans. The battle was fought in the Gulf of Patras, with the Christian forces vastly outnumbered and underequipped. As the battle waged, Pope Pius V directed all the faithful to pray the Rosary for a Christian victory. Miraculously, the Christians won the battle and Christendom was saved. In commemoration of this amazing victory, Pope Pius V added the title *Auxilium Christianorum* (Help of Christians) to the Litany of Loreto.[2]

REFLECTION

Each of us has our own battles to fight, in which we face insurmountable odds and perhaps even grave danger. It could be anything from conquering a bad habit to enduring persecution, but they are battles just the same. Anything that threatens to separate us from God or deter us from doing his will is a battle. In these battles, we need to call in reinforcements to help us stay strong and fight courageously. Our Blessed Mother Mary, Help of Christians, is our reinforcement, and she will help us obtain the victory.

PRAYER

Mary, Help of Christians, I need your help. I so often face battles that make life more difficult for me, and I weaken easily. Be my help, my protection, and my source of strength. Amen.

Queen of Angels

He has inspired her, even since the days of the earthly paradise — though she existed then only in his idea — with so much hatred against that accursed enemy of God, with so much ingenuity in unveiling the malice of that ancient serpent, with so much power to conquer, to overthrow and to crush that proud, impious rebel, that he fears her not only more than all angels and men, but in a sense more than God himself.

St. Louis de Montfort, *True Devotion to Mary*

In the Book of Revelation, chapter 12, we see Mary as the woman clothed with the sun, with the moon under her feet and a crown of twelve stars on her head. In Saint John's vision, she is pregnant and crying out with birth pangs. As she struggles to give birth, a great red dragon with seven heads and ten horns and seven diadems on his heads appears, and with his tail sweeps away one-third of the stars in heaven, throwing them down to earth. The dragon then stands before the woman, planning to devour her child as soon as it is born. Then the woman gives birth to a son who is to rule all the nations with a "rod of iron" (Rv 12:5). Quickly, the child was snatched away from her and taken to God's throne while the woman fled into the wilderness, to a place prepared for her by God. At that moment, a war broke out in heaven, and Saint Michael and his angels fought against the dragon and his angels. The good angels defeated the evil angels and threw them down to the earth.

There is a lot going on in this dramatic scene! But there are two points that should draw our focus here: First, Mary (the woman clothed with the sun) wears a crown of twelve stars, signaling her queenship. Second, she is served by the angels, who rush to her aid and fight the demons who threaten her and her child. This demonstrates the royal place Mary holds above all the angels — both the good angels and the fallen ones. Mary reigns as queen above the angels who, by God's design, are subject to her since she is the mother of God and holds a place higher than theirs in the kingdom of heaven.

This is even more remarkable when we consider that there are nine choirs of good angels, each choir numbering more than can be counted. All the choirs — seraphim, cherubim, thrones, dominions, virtues, powers, principalities, archangels, and angels — serve her with complete devotion. Each choir has its own characteristics and responsibilities, and each angel within that choir is unique. No other queen in history or to come has a realm of that magnitude. Thus the heavenly Father has given Mary a place of highest honor both in heaven and on earth. She is unequivocally the everlasting Queen of Angels.

REFLECTION

The image of the Blessed Virgin Mary in the Book of Revelation is quite different from the images of her presented in other works.

In Revelation, she is both vulnerable and powerful as she stands radiant with the sun, crowned with twelve stars, and the moon under her feet. It would be good for us to consider what this image means for us in our personal lives. Who is Mary to you?

PRAYER

Queen of Angels, my dearest Mother Mary, help me to understand your queenly power. Show me how to give you the honor you deserve in your singular and royal position. Amen.

Queen of Patriarchs

She has surpassed the riches of the virgins, the confessors, the martyrs, the apostles, the prophets, the patriarchs, and the angels, for she herself is the first fruit of the virgins, the mirror of confessors, the rose of martyrs, the ruler of apostles, the oracle of prophets, the daughter of patriarchs, the queen of angels.

Saint Bonaventure

In the fifth chapter of Genesis, we find a list of ten patriarchs who lived before the Great Flood: Adam, Seth, Enosh, Kenan, Mahalalel, Jared, Enoch, Methuselah, Lamech, and Noah. In the eleventh chapter of Genesis, we find patriarchs who lived after the flood: Shem, Arpachshad, Shelah, Eber, Peleg, Reu, Serug, Nahor, Terah, and Abram (later Abraham), Isaac, and Jacob. The twelve sons of Jacob also are considered patriarchs and are a type of the Twelve Apostles who would come later. They are Reuben, Simeon, Levi, Judah, Issachar, Zebulun, Benjamin, Dan, Naphtali, Gad, Asher, and Joseph. The patriarchs of the Old Testament were the first to be obedient to God's will and to demonstrate exceptional faith in God. They are the founding fathers of both Judaism and Christianity and play a vital role in the history of the People of God. Early Christians, and even Our Lord himself, often invoked the patriarchs, relying on their teaching and example and petitioning their guidance. Their stories are important to us because they show the richness of our Christian faith.[1]

The patriarchs received and cared for the Old Covenant, which eventually led to the New Covenant in Christ. Their stories are more than just stories; they are lessons for the generations to follow. Although they had their faults and made mistakes, the patriarchs are examples of fidelity and obedience to God. Of all the patriarchs, Abraham is held as the patriarch par excellence, frequently invoked by the prophets. He is the father of many nations, which means he is also our father, and he is a symbol of firm belief and righteousness. He was specially chosen by God for a mission that would impact the entire world.

Yet, as great as the patriarchs were, Our Lady is greater. She is their queen and ours. She reigns supreme over the patriarchs in her wisdom, righteousness, faith, and obedience to God. Like Abraham, she is the parent of many nations, since Jesus has asked her to be mother of all peoples. Without Mary, we would not have the God-Man, nor would we have his Mystical Body, the Church. Because of Mary, we have the traditions of our Faith and the salvation they provide. From heaven, the patriarchs look upon her with immense joy and reverence, knowing that she is far greater than they could ever be. Mary, Queen of Patriarchs, is their queen and ours.

REFLECTION

Our Lord Jesus invoked the patriarchs and looked to them with respect. In spite of their imperfections, their fidelity paved the way for the Messiah. Mary's fiat was the culmination of all their suffering and striving, and now she reigns in heaven as their queen as well as ours.

PRAYER

O Queen of Patriarchs, I do not know the patriarchs as I would like to and perhaps as I ought. Teach me, please, what is important to know about them so that I may learn from their obedience, righteousness, and faith. Amen.

Queen of Prophets

My soul magnifies the Lord,
and my spirit rejoices in God my Savior,
for he has looked with favor on
the lowliness of his servant.
Surely, from now on all generations
will call me blessed;
for the Mighty One has done great things for me,
and holy is his name.

Luke 1:46–49

According to the *Catechism*, a prophet is one sent by God to form the people of the Old Covenant in hope of salvation (see 64). Paging through the Bible, we can see that many of the Old Testament books were written by prophets. According to Scripture scholars, there are four major prophets and twelve minor prophets. The major prophets are called such because of the number of their prophecies, and they likely are familiar to you: Isaiah, Jeremiah, Ezekiel, and Daniel. You may also recognize some of the names of the minor prophets: Hosea, Joel,

Amos, Obadiah, Jonah, Micah, Nahum, Habakkuk, Zephaniah, Haggai, Zechariah, and Malachi. The prophets are a major part of the history of the People of God, including us.

The main reason for the prophets' existence and mission was to point to the coming of the Messiah. All things converge on Christ, and his coming was so important that God prepared his people over the course of centuries, persistently trying to awaken their hearts in readiness. As the *Catechism* tells us:

> The coming of God's Son is an event of such immensity that God willed to prepare for it over centuries. He makes everything converge on Christ: all the rituals and sacrifices, figures, and symbols of the "First Covenant." He announces them through the mouths of the prophets who succeeded one another in Israel. Moreover, he awakens in the hearts of the pagans a dim expectation of this coming. (522)

John the Baptist was the last of the prophets of the Old Covenant, and he was greatly respected and honored by Our Lord, who said of him:

> Truly I tell you, among those born of women no one has arisen greater than John the Baptist; yet the least in the kingdom of heaven is greater than he. From the days of John the Baptist until now the kingdom of heaven has suffered violence, and the violent take it by force. For all the prophets and the law prophesied until John came; and if you are willing to accept it, he is Elijah who is to come. Let anyone with ears listen! (Matthew 11:11–15)

John the Baptist was the last of the Old Covenant prophets, and we could say that Mary was the first prophet of the New

Covenant. Her first prophecy occurred at the Visitation when she prayed her Magnificat (see Lk 1:47–55).

She prophesied again at the wedding at Cana when she told the servants, "Do whatever he tells you" (Jn 2:5). This was more than an utterance for that time and place, it was a prediction of Our Lord's first public miracle and a credo for us to live by. Although we have no record of her words during Jesus' passion and death, Mary's very being and actions were a prophecy, giving witness to the fact that his suffering and hers must be endured so that all mankind could be saved.

The prophets of the Old Testament proclaimed a radical redemption of the People of God and purification from their infidelities resulting in salvation for all nations. Mary is the descendent of the holy women of the Bible — women like Sarah, Rebecca, Rachel, Miriam, Deborah, Hannah, Judith, and Esther — who promoted the promise of salvation (see CCC 64). Mary was part of the fulfillment of the promise of salvation, and in that way she could be considered the greatest of all the prophets. She is indeed the Queen of Prophets.

REFLECTION

Mary's work as prophetess has continued throughout time. At every one of her apparitions — Lourdes, Fátima, Champion, Akita, Kibeho, La Sallette, and more — she came with a warning and plea for conversion just like the prophets of old. Her words are not empty; they always point us back to her son. Although these approved apparitions are private revelation, and we are not required to believe them, her words contain much wisdom for us if we are willing to study and heed them.

PRAYER

Queen of Prophets, please help me to understand and heed the words of the prophets, especially yours. Call me to radical redemption and purification of my infidelities so that I can spend eternity in heaven with you and your son. Amen.

Queen of Apostles

No one has access to the Almighty as his mother has; none has merit such as hers. Her son will deny her nothing that she asks; and herein lies her power. While she defends the Church, neither height nor depth, neither men nor evil spirits, neither great monarchs, nor craft of man, nor popular violence, can avail to harm us; for human life is short, but Mary reigns above, a queen forever.

St. John Henry Newman

Our Lady was the first of Jesus' apostles in the sense that she was the first to hear the Good News and share it with others. At the Annunciation, she was greeted by the Archangel Gabriel, who proclaimed that she had been chosen to become the mother of God. After ascertaining that this would not affect her private vow of virginity, she gave her wholehearted yes to the motherhood of Christ and all that would entail. Her next step was to visit her cousin Elizabeth and share the good news with her. While pregnant with Jesus, she embarked on her journey of apostleship.

As Our Lord grew, she cared for him, listened to him, learned from him, and accompanied him throughout his ministry. She never wavered from following God's will exactly and never doubted his providence. All that she did and said echoed the words and actions of the Messiah. Through the years, she came to know Our Lord's apostles, and I can imagine that she loved and mothered them as she had loved and mothered her son. We know from the early traditions of Marian devotion that the apostles loved her in return, honoring her because she was Jesus' mother but also because she was grace-filled and lovable. During Jesus' passion and death, it was Mary who remained by his side, Mary who succumbed to God's will, hard though it was, without resistance. She did what the apostles should have done during that time, walking the path to Calvary with Jesus and standing at the foot of the cross as he suffered and died. Mary remained by Our Lord's side throughout his life and death.

After Jesus' death, the apostles gathered again, at first to comfort each other and then to spend time with the Risen Christ. After his ascension, the apostles gathered in the Upper Room to await the coming of the Paraclete. Some of Jesus' relatives gathered there as well, along with certain women and Mary. Mary would have been the center of attention, as she was the last remaining connection to the Lord. The apostles would have looked to her for comfort and direction, which she of course gave to them. When the Spirit came, he filled everyone present with strength, courage, zeal, and wisdom so that they could begin their mission of founding the ancient Church. I believe in my heart that some of their courage, strength, and zeal came from our Mother Mary. How proud she must have been! How elated she must have been at their bravery and enthusiasm! Mary — the first and most perfect of the apostles — now took her place among the faithful as Queen of the Apostles.

REFLECTION

We honor the apostles on feast days, in the liturgy, and at holy places dedicated to them. But do we honor them with our words and deeds? Do we strive to be true and faithful apostles in our daily lives? This is our calling, and we must turn to the Queen of Apostles for her intercession so that we, too, can be strong, courageous, and zealous in living the Good News and sharing it with others.

PRAYER

Mary, Queen of Apostles, pray for me so that I can be as strong, courageous, and zealous as you were and as the Twelve were after Pentecost. Pray for me to receive the Holy Spirit as they did, and show me the way to true apostleship in Christ so that I may effectively lead others to him. Amen.

QUEEN OF MARTYRS

Meanwhile let us feed upon the honey of those pious instructions left to us by holy men of old and let us beseech God to give us the wings of the dove, so that we may not only fly in this present life, but also find our rest in the eternity of that which is to come.

St. Francis de Sales

Some years ago, while I was working on my book *My Queen, My Mother: A Marian Pilgrimage Across America*, I visited the Our Lady of Martyrs Shrine in Auriesville, New York, built on the site of what was once the Mohawk village of Ossernenon. It marks the place of martyrdom of three of the eight North American martyrs: Fr. Isaac Jogues and his two lay companions, René Goupil and John LaLande. These brave men were martyred in the 1640s, as were five Jesuit priests in Canada. They had come from France to America via Canada in the early 1600s, intent on converting the Native Americans to Christianity. The greatest danger they faced were the fearsome Iroquois, which was a federation of the Mohawk, Oneida, Onondaga, Cayuga, and Seneca tribes. This federation was brutal to its enemies and exterminated any tribe that refused to submit to its dominance. At the time, the Iroquois were at war with the Hurons and Algonquins — two tribes who were allied with the French. The Iroquois considered the French their enemies, since the French held growing influence around the Great Lakes region. And so, the French missionaries were considered enemies as well.[1]

While traveling, Fr. Jogues and his companions were ambushed and taken to the Iroquois camp along with forty other missionaries, eighteen of whom were killed almost immediately. Over a two-week period, the captives were taken from village to village, each time being brutalized by running the gauntlet, burning, torture, mutilation, and more. The prisoners were divided and sent to separate camps where the villagers would routinely strip them naked, club them, gnaw their fingers and hands to a pulp, burn their flesh with lighted torches, toss hot coals on their exposed bodies, pull out their hair and beards by roots, reopen their wounds, and worse. Somehow, Fr. Jogues and his companions survived, praying the Rosary together daily — the first recitation of the Rosary documented was in what would become New York State.[2]

There was a ravine just down the hill from the village, where the prisoners were made to work. One day René Goupil was observed teaching the Sign of the Cross, and it was mistaken for a curse. Consequently, a Mohawk grabbed Goupil and split his skull with a tomahawk. His body was dumped into the ravine and was later found by Fr. Jogues. Despite his efforts to bury the body, it was lost forever when the ravine flooded. Eventually, Fr. Jogues and John LaLande also were killed by the Mohawks.[3] As I walked the ravine during my visit, I could feel the presence and courage of those who had died for their faith. This was a sacred place, and the ground I stood upon was holy ground, soaked by the blood of the martyrs. I thought of their heroism and the horrors they had endured, and I sobbed.

Like so many martyrs before and after them, Fr. Isaac Jogues and his companions looked to our Blessed Mother for consolation and courage. The Rosary became a lifeline for them as they prayed it repeatedly in petition for endurance and protection and hope of rescue. Our Lady — who experienced her own mystical martyrdom during her son's crucifixion — has a special place in her heart for martyrs. They gave their all for Jesus, as she did. She accompanies them in their suffering to the point of suffering with them because of her love for them. She will lead them to the ultimate victory, and for all these reasons, she is the Queen of Martyrs.

REFLECTION

We may or may not be called to physical martyrdom, but we must be ready for it. Many of us will be called to what is known as a "white martyrdom," which is exceptional suffering during our lifetime but without a bloody death. Either way, the Queen of Martyrs will accompany us to the victory if we remain close and rely on her.

PRAYER

Queen of Martyrs, you understand the suffering of the martyrs because of your own suffering. You understand my suffering, too. I may never be called to die for my faith, but I want to be courageous enough to do just that. Pray for me to endure whatever God may ask of me. Amen.

Queen of Confessors

The most Holy Virgin places herself between her Son and us. The greater sinners we are, the more tenderness and compassion does she feel for us. The child that has cost its mother most tears is the dearest to her heart.

St. John Vianney

When we hear the word *confessor*, we usually think of the priest in the confessional administering the Sacrament of Reconciliation. There are many saintly confessors who were heroic in their virtue and dedicated to their office. Among them are St. John Vianney (d. 1859), St. Pio of Pietrelcina (d. 1968), and St. Josemaría Escrivá (d. 1975). Biographies of the saints tell us that St. John Vianney would spend up to sixteen hours a day hearing confessions, and Padre Pio often spent at least eight hours a day in the confessional. And countless other holy priests, who go unrecognized, valiantly spend hours upon hours hearing confessions.

But there is another kind of confessor that we must consider.

Heroes of the Faith who publicly professed Christ in times of persecution — facing imprisonment, torture, exile, or hard labor — yet remained faithful all their lives were called Confessors. They differ from the martyrs in that they were not murdered for the Faith but died of illness, calamity, or natural causes.

Mary also is a confessor, as she professed the Faith throughout her earthly life and continues to do so from heaven until this day. We could even consider her the first confessor. She professed the Faith through her pregnancy; by bringing the Christ into the world; by helping Saint Joseph raise Jesus and prepare him for his adult life and ministry; and by being a steadfast witness during Jesus' passion and death. Her words are only recorded a few times in the Bible, and all were professions of faith, from her Magnificat to the Finding in the Temple and the Wedding at Cana. Intuitively, we know that Mary spoke many other times that are not recorded in Scripture, professing and sharing her deep faith. As she was the most perfect of all the apostles, Mary is also the most perfect of all the Confessors of the Church, making her the Queen of Confessors.

REFLECTION

Whether they be priests in the confessional or men and women of heroic virtue who professed the Faith in spite of great hardship, all confessors are vital to the Church. We would be lost without them! And so, we must be grateful for them and pray for them daily — especially our priestly confessors.

PRAYER

Mary, Queen of Confessors, I would like to live a life of heroic virtue as the Confessors of the Church did. Sadly, I often fall short of that ideal. Help me, please, to frequently cleanse my soul through the Sacrament of Reconciliation, to gain what knowledge I can of the Church and her teachings, and to valiantly profess the Faith throughout my life. Amen.

Queen of Virgins

In Mary, there was nothing unsurrendered, nothing lost; there was a harvest without the loss of the bud; an autumn in an eternal spring; a submission without spoliation. Virgin and Mother!

Ven. Fulton Sheen, The World's First Love[1]

In our secular and disordered culture, virginity is all too often seen as a form of deprivation. It is assumed that the lack of sexual experience means either that someone is unattractive or the victim of unfortunate circumstances. For some, virginity is an embarrassment. Not so in the Church. The Church values virginity as a symbol of purity and an asset to be valued. In biblical times, virgins were protected and considered desirable spouses, even for kings (see, for example, Esther 2:2–3). There were holy individuals — like Mary — who took perpetual vows of virginity, pledging themselves entirely to God. Many virgins are mentioned in the canon of the Mass, most notably Saints Perpetua, Agatha, Lucy, Agnes, Cecilia, and Anastasia, all of whom were martyred in defense of their chastity.[2] It is worth mentioning here that there also were male virgins among the saints and martyrs. However, males who refrain from sexual relationships are considered celibate, while women who make the same choice are referred to as virgins.

Within the early Church there were both men and women who lived consecrated virginity. Over time, a solemn rite was formulated, by which women would consecrate themselves to God, representing the Church as Bride of Christ. Gradually this practice was used only by orders of contemplative nuns, but in 1970 things changed. The rite was revised, allowing the diocesan bishop to consecrate both nuns and women living in the world. According to the Code of Canon Law, these women became part of "the order of virgins who, expressing the holy resolution of following Christ more closely, are consecrated to God by the diocesan bishop according to the approved liturgical right, are mystically betrothed to Christ, the Son of God, and are dedicated to the service of the Church."[3]

Thus, virginity in its purest form has become a beautiful vocation for women, following in the footsteps of the virgins of the early Church. One of those virgins, of course, is our Blessed Mother Mary. Not only is she *a* virgin, but she is *the* virgin, and in her, the vocations of virginity and motherhood are bonded. As Ven. Fulton Sheen wrote in his book *The World's First Love*, "Virginity and maternity are not so irreconcilable as it would seem. Every virgin yearns to become a mother, either physically or spiritually, for unless she creates, mothers, nurses, and fosters life, her heart is as uneasy and awkward as a giant ship in shallow waters. She has the vocation of generating life, either in the flesh or in the spirit through conversion."[4] Mary, virgin and mother, is the model for all women and the inspiration for all virgins, for she is the Queen of Virgins.

REFLECTION

We all are called to be pure according to our state in life. Those called to consecrated virginity give themselves totally to God and are an inspiration to those of us who are not consecrated virgins. We can learn from them the ideal of self-gift — giving of ourselves to others in a holy way that is pure and God-centered. That is what Mary did best of all.

PRAYER

Mary, I honor you as Queen of Virgins and want to have a virginal heart like yours. Protect me from the temptations of impurity and show me how to give my life entirely to God. Amen.

Queen of All Saints

The Church is holy: the Most Holy God is her author; Christ, her bridegroom, gave himself up to make her holy; the Spirit of holiness gives her life. Since she still includes sinners, she is "the sinless one made up of sinners." Her holiness shines in the saints; in Mary she is already all-holy.

CCC 867

I am moved to tears every time I hear the Litany of the Saints sung, even when I am listening to it on a podcast platform or music app. During special masses (Holy Saturday, the Saturday before Pentecost, priestly and diaconate ordinations, confirmations, and on some solemnities), you will find me, tissues in hand, stifling snuffles during the litany. It moves me for two reasons. First, the melody and the way it is usually sung with cantor and congregational responses is aesthetically beautiful. Second, the names of the saints mentioned one after another in solemn veneration is a reminder to me of those who have gone before us and lived exceptional and exemplary lives for the sake of Our Lord. As the chant progresses, I picture the saints gathered and giving praise and worship to God on his heavenly throne and the Father looking lovingly down on them. I am familiar with most of them, many of whom share names with people I know and who are dear to me. This, too, pulls at my heartstrings, because these holy and outstandingly courageous men and women lived, taught, suffered, and died, not only for love of God, but also for love of me and all those whom I love.

When we pray the Creed, we profess our faith in the Communion of Saints. The *Catechism* teaches us that the Church is an assembly of all the saints, including those who already are in heaven, those who are striving for holiness here on earth, and those to come. The Communion of Saints is nourished and strengthened by the holy Eucharist, or Communion, which binds us together in Christ and strengthens us as his mystical body (see CCC 948). It is awesome to think that we are united with the saints in the Church. Furthermore, our dear Blessed Mother also is part of the Communion of Saints, meaning that we are united with her in the Body of Christ.

We do not always think of Mary as a saint, but she is just that. Turning once again to the *Catechism*, we learn that a saint is "the 'holy one' who leads a life in union with God through the grace of Christ and receives the reward of eternal life" (CCC Glossary). Doesn't that perfectly describe the Blessed Mother? What is more, Mary was preserved from the consequences of original sin and so had no faults, unlike the other saints who were sinners. The saints look to her for example, protection, and intercession. That is why Mary is Queen of All Saints.

REFLECTION

We are tangible and sensory creatures, prone to be affected by our environment and what we see and hear. That is why it is critical that we surround ourselves with the good, the true, and the beautiful. We should meditate upon the saints, particularly those who have touched our lives in some way.

PRAYER

O Mary, Queen of All Saints, pray for me. I am not the saint that I would like to be! Show me what I need to purge from my life and pray for me to be open to the grace God wants to give me to help me move closer and closer to sanctity. Amen.

Queen Conceived without Original Sin

Thou art that only one in whom the Savior found his rest, and with whom he has deposited all his treasures. Hence all the world, O Mary, honors thy chaste womb, as the temple of God, where the salvation of the world had its beginning.

St. Bernard of Clairvaux

Original sin is a tricky subject. Unless we understand God's goodness and mercy, the consequences of original sin may seem like cruelty. It is far from that. Saint Paul tells us, "Therefore, just as sin came into the world through one man, and death came through sin, and so death spread to all because all have sinned — sin was indeed in the world before the law, but sin is not reckoned when there is no law" (Rom 5:12–13). Paul's point was that Adam and Eve broke God's law by eating from the Tree of the Knowledge of Good and Evil when he had specifically forbidden them to do so. Whenever a law is broken, there must be consequences, and so all who came after our first parents had upon their souls the stain — or effects — of that original sin. Their action had changed all of creation and God's plan for it. However, in his divine providence God also had a plan for our redemption, and that plan was to send his only-begotten Son to bear the consequences for us through his passion and death. As Paul explained, we have been justified by Christ's blood and saved by him from the wrath of God (see Rom 5:9).

The doctrine of original sin is found in Sacred Scripture. For example, in Ecclesiastes, we read that "there is no one on earth so righteous as to do good without ever sinning" (Eccl 7:20). The saints also taught about original sin. In his *Summa Theologiae*, St. Thomas Aquinas confirmed the doctrine of original sin and its impact on mankind. He wrote, "According to the Catholic Faith we must firmly believe that Christ alone excepted, all men descended from Adam contract original sin from him; else all would not need redemption."[1] Yes, we all need redemption.

It might surprise you to know that Mary also needed redemption. After all, she was human and part of mankind. But to become the mother of the Savior, it was necessary that she be entirely filled by God's grace. Before Christ could dwell in her womb, there could be no stain of sin nor any effects of original sin. The Church teaches that Mary was completely full of grace (the reason Gabriel addressed her as such) and was redeemed from the moment of her conception. Some refer to this as her having been "pre-redeemed." That is what the dogma of the Immaculate Conception proclaims. When Blessed Pope Pius IX proclaimed the dogma in 1854, he wrote: "The most Blessed Virgin Mary was, from the first moment of her conception, by a singular grace and privilege of almighty God and by virtue of the merits of Jesus Christ, Savior of the human race, preserved immune from all stain of original sin."[2]

There can be no more concise description of Mary's privileged position in the economy of salvation. And so, she rightfully bears the title, Queen Conceived without Original Sin.

REFLECTION

The dogma of the Immaculate Conception can be difficult to understand and is one that our non-Catholic brethren tend to criticize and negate. We must strive to understand it clearly for ourselves and be able to charitably explain it to others in honor of our mother and queen.

PRAYER

O Mary, you alone are immaculately conceived, and you deserve to be honored for it. Help me, please, to understand your Immaculate Conception and be able to draw others to you as the Queen Conceived without Original Sin. Amen.

Queen Assumed into Heaven

"Although the body was duly buried, it did not remain in the state of death, neither was it dissolved by decay. … You were transferred to your heavenly home, O Lady, Queen and Mother of God in truth."

St. John Damascene

Have you ever wondered why there are no first-class relics of Mary? It is because she was assumed into heaven, body and soul. And how do we know this? Since apostolic times, the Tomb of Mary has been a sacred place close to Mount Zion, at the top of which is a spot marked as the "Dormition of Mary" (or the "Falling Asleep of Mary"). The dogma of the Assumption was clarified at the Council of Chalcedon in 451. Bishops from throughout the Mediterranean world gathered in Constantinople, and one of their topics was the belief that Mary was assumed into heaven. Emperor Marcian had requested that the Patriarch of Jerusalem bring the relics of Mary to Constantinople during the council so that they could be enshrined in the capital. The patriarch explained to the emperor that there were no relics of Mary in Jerusalem because, "Mary had died in the presence of the apostles; but her tomb, when opened later … was found empty and so the apostles concluded that the body was taken up into heaven."[1]

When I was in Jerusalem on a press junket some years ago, I visited the Church of the Dormition of Mary, which rests on the spot of Mary's tomb. It was a surreal experience. There was a life-size statue of Mary lying as if on a burial slab, but she was beautifully dressed and radiant, lying peacefully with eyes closed and hands folded, surrounded by flowers. I know it was just a statue, but it gave me the feeling of standing over Mary's holy body — the same body that once held our Lord Jesus Christ. I imagined what it must have been like for the apostles to visit their mother's tomb, only to find it completely empty. In my heart's imagination, I could sense their sadness but also their wonder and elation at realizing what this meant. There could be only one answer: Mary had been assumed into heaven!

This makes perfect sense to me. How could the body that held the Savior be allowed to become corrupted? How could it be allowed to remain in a tomb? No, the body of Mary must be preserved and completely united with her soul. That body would have to be kept whole, holy, and full of life. There is another aspect of this to consider. God knew from all eternity that, after Mary's death, he would need her to appear to human beings to bring to them the messages of her son. In all the Marian apparitions, she is completely visible to the seers and obviously alive. This seems to indicate that her body was not allowed to remain buried and decay like all other human bodies. The *Catechism* offers an exceptional explanation:

> "Finally, the Immaculate Virgin, preserved free from all stain of original sin, when the course of her earthly life was

finished, was taken up body and soul into heavenly glory, and exalted by the Lord as Queen over all things, so that she might be the more fully conformed to her son, the Lord of lords and conqueror of sin and death." The Assumption of the Blessed Virgin is a singular participation in her son's Resurrection and an anticipation of the resurrection of other Christians:

> In giving birth you kept your virginity; in your Dormition you did not leave the world, O Mother of God, but were joined to the source of Life. You conceived the living God and, by your prayers, will deliver our souls from death. (CCC 966)

REFLECTION

There is no human body aside from the body of Jesus as holy as Mary's because she was immaculately conceived, and she bore within her womb the Christ. Of course, our bodies cannot be as holy, but we can and should strive to keep our bodies holy in imitation of the Queen Assumed into Heaven — and in anticipation of our own hoped-for resurrection at the end of time.

PRAYER

O Mary, Queen Assumed into Heaven, how I long to see you, body and soul! Pray for me, that I may live a life of excellence and devotion to God so that I may one day be united with you in heaven. Amen.

Queen of the Most Holy Rosary

There is no sinner in the world, however much at enmity with God, who cannot recover God's grace by recourse to Mary, and by asking her assistance.

St. Bridget of Sweden

I have heard the Rosary referred to as a catechism in beads. The four groups of mysteries with five mysteries each depict the lives of Jesus, Mary, and Saint Joseph, with particular emphasis on the life of Jesus. Many who do not understand think that the Rosary is a form of worship of Mary and therefore idolatrous. That could not be further from the truth. Catholics do not worship Mary, and the Rosary is a form of meditation on Jesus, not a glorification of Mary. In fact, the Rosary is specifically Christ-centered. Even the decades that focus on Mary do so only because she is the mother of Jesus.

That is not to say that we do not honor Mary by praying the Rosary. It was Our Lady who presented the Rosary to Saint

Dominic and instructed him to pray it and spread its devotion throughout the world. It was 1214, and the Albigensian heresy threatened the Church. The Rosary was a valuable tool to counter this heresy, since it taught the Gospels and truths of the Faith. When she appeared to Saint Dominic, she asked him, "Dear Dominic, do you know which weapon the Blessed Trinity wants to use to reform the world?" Dominic responded, "Oh, my Lady, you know far better than I do, because next to your son Jesus Christ you have always been the chief instrument of our salvation." To this Mary replied: "I want you to know that, in this kind of warfare, the principal weapon has always been the Angelic Psalter (Rosary), which is the foundation-stone of the New Testament. Therefore, if you want to reach these hardened souls and win them over to God, preach my Psalter."[1]

Through the centuries, the Rosary has been a treasured form of prayer and meditation. In his book *The Secret of the Rosary*, St. Louis de Montfort quoted Pope Leo XI as saying, "We have elsewhere brought it to the attention of the devout Christian that not least among the advantages of the Rosary is the ready means it puts in his hands to nourish his faith, and to keep him from ignorance of his religion and the danger of error."[2] De Montfort relates the story of an Albigensian who was possessed by the devil. Saint Dominic exorcised the man, and the devils who were in possession of him were forced to answer the saint's questions. They told him that there were fifteen thousand of them in the man, and that by preaching the Rosary, Dominic put fear and horror into the very depths of hell, so that he was the man they hated most throughout the entire world because of the souls he was saving through the Rosary. Saint Dominic put his rosary around the possessed man's neck and asked the devils to tell him who, of all the saints in heaven, was the one they feared most. After much wailing, screaming, and pleading, they finally answered him. The one they feared most and that caused them the most pain was the Blessed Virgin Mary and the power of the Rosary.[3]

REFLECTION

It was Mary who brought the Rosary to humanity, and Mary who continues to ask us to pray to it, as she has said in many of her apparitions. The Rosary continues to be a valuable tool to counter heresies and protect us from evil. Mary, Queen of the Most Holy Rosary, has asked this of us for the sake of our salvation.

PRAYER

O Queen of the Most Holy Rosary, show me how to be as devoted to you and to your Rosary as Saint Dominic was. Let me be a champion of the Rosary, in accordance with your request. Amen.

QUEEN OF FAMILIES

Assuredly, she who played the part of the Creator's servant and mother is in all strictness and truth in reality God's mother and lady and queen over all created things.

St. John Damascene

When our children were young, we crowned the Blessed Mother as Queen of Our Family, an adaptation of the Catholic custom of crowning Mary during the month of May. But for us, this was not just for the month of May; it was for a lifetime. We wanted her to reign as queen over our family, home, property, employment, education, and recreation. We wanted her to rule over every aspect of our lives as a family — to protect, guide, educate, console, and sustain us always. I even fashioned a plaster crown, decorated it with gold paint and colored jewels, and attached a hook to the back. Then our family worked together to write our own crowning prayer and held a formal crowning celebration. We attached the crown to the frame of her painting in our prayer corner, positioned right above her head. Together, we prayed our prayer aloud. Since then, we have been aware that we are "ruled" by a holy Queen, turning to her in times of need, confusion, sorrow, and joy. Our family has been through some incredibly difficult times and each time, Mary has revealed herself as victorious.

Mary knew the ups and downs of family life. She and Saint Joseph worked hard for everything they had and were never of great means. The two of them cared for Jesus and did their best to bring him up to be a fine and noble man. The Holy Family lived, ate, slept, laughed, cried, rejoiced, worked, learned, and played together. They shared the trials, concerns, and uncertainties of other families and knew the same kinds of joys and sorrows they did. Based merely on human observation, they were a normal, average family living a normal, average life. However, they were that and more. This family of Nazareth had a king and queen among its members. Jesus was (and is) the King of Kings. Mary was (and is) the Queen of Heaven. Albeit in the humblest of ways, Mary reigned as queen over the Holy Family.

Yet her queenship does not end there. Mary is also mother and queen of the Church. The Church teaches that the family is a "domestic church" because it is within the family that the seed of faith is planted and is nourished by the teaching and good example of parents. The family is the smallest cell of the Church and therefore part of the Mystical Body of Christ. Family not only forms the basis for the Church, but for all of society as well.

In his apostolic exhortation *Familiaris Consortio*, Pope St. John Paul II wrote:

> May the Virgin Mary, who is the Mother of the Church, also be the Mother of "the Church of the home." Thanks to her motherly aid, may each Christian family really become a "little Church" in which the mystery of the Church of Christ is mirrored and given new life. May

> she, the Handmaid of the Lord, be an example of humble and generous acceptance of the will of God. May she, the Sorrowful Mother at the foot of the cross, comfort the sufferings and dry the tears of those in distress because of the difficulties of their families.[1]

REFLECTION

Mary is queen of the Church, of which the domestic church is a part. The domestic church is the family, a sacred institution willed by God. We can only conclude that Mary is the Queen of Families, and we can ask her to reign over our families.

PRAYER

Mary, Queen of Families, my own family is imperfect and subject to brokenness. I want my family to resemble the Holy Family, with you as its queen. Please help us. Amen.

Queen of Peace

Above all, clothe yourselves with love, which binds everything together in perfect harmony. And let the peace of Christ rule in your hearts, to which indeed you were called in the one body. And be thankful.

Colossians 3:14–15

Queen of Peace. Pope Benedict XV inserted this title of Mary into the Litany of Loreto in 1917, during the horror of World War I.[1] With war raging on many fronts, the world was in desperate need of peace. And because it was such a complicated war, the only way peace could be achieved was through divine intervention. It is no wonder, then, that Mary chose to appear to Lucia, Jacinta, and Francisco in Fátima, Portugal, in 1917. She had many lessons for the children, and many prophecies for them to share with the world. She also issued to them an urgent request to pray for peace.

She told them, "I want you to come on the thirteenth day of next month and to continue to pray the Rosary every day in honor of Our Lady of the Rosary, in order to obtain peace for the world and the end of the war, for she alone can help." Mary told the children that if people did what she asked, many souls would be saved, and there would be peace. If not, however, Russia would spread its errors throughout the world, and there would be more wars and persecutions of the Church. The good would be martyred, she told them, the pope would have to suffer much, and nations would be destroyed.[2]

Mary also gave instructions to Jacinta a few years after the original Fátima apparitions. She said:

> Tell everybody that God gives graces through the Immaculate Heart of Mary. Tell them to ask graces from her, and that the Heart of Jesus wishes to be venerated together with the Immaculate Heart of Mary. Ask them to plead for peace from the Immaculate Heart of Mary, for the Lord has confided the peace of the world to her.[3]

REFLECTION

There have been other times in which Mary instructed the faithful to pray for peace, pointing to herself as the instrument and intercessor of that peace. These were not acts of pride; they were acts of humility and obedience to God's will. She made it quite clear that she was not the originator of peace, but that her Immaculate Heart was the channel for the peace of Christ. His peace is not of this world. He told his disciples, "Peace I leave with you; my peace I give to you. I do not give to you as the world gives. Do not let your hearts be troubled, and do not let them be afraid" (Jn 14:27). This is the kind of peace that comes to us from Christ through Mary. In this way, he has given her the honor of being Queen of Peace.

PRAYER

Mary, please be Queen of Peace over me. Fill me with the peace of your son and surround me with your motherly peace when I am troubled or in distress. Help me to be an instrument of peace for others in my life. Amen.

Conclusion

The Litany of Loreto invites us to come inside Mary's heart as if we were entering the home of someone dear to us. When you enter the home of a loved one, you cross the threshold filled with good memories of previous times together and in joyful anticipation of more such cherished moments. Once inside, you never want to leave. Mary's heart is indeed our home, and she awaits us there, eager to spend cherished moments with us in an atmosphere of love and joy. Upon entering, we will never want to leave.

The Litany of Loreto is like the home of Mary's heart in another way, also. When you visit a loved one, your eyes slowly pass over your surroundings, and you notice all the little things that are present in the home. The surroundings, furnishings, ornamentation, and environment of the home show you who the person is and what they are really like. A wise priest once told me that unless you know a person's home, you do not know the person. This is true. The titles of the litany are like the surroundings, furnishings, ornamentation, and environment of Mary's home, and they show us who Mary is and what she is really like.

As our eyes pass over our surroundings, we notice all the little things — the meanings and implications of the various titles of our Mother Mary — and we come to know her in a very tangible way and in all the aspects of her being.

There is a common expression, "don't be a stranger," meaning that you should return soon and visit often. I encourage you not to be a stranger in the Blessed Mother's home. Come back soon and visit the Litany of Loreto often. Mary is there, with open arms and yearning heart, to welcome you and invite you in.

Acknowledgments

Special thanks to the folks at OSV Books for inviting me to write *Mother Most Powerful*. It has been my joy and privilege!

Special thanks, too, to my husband and amazing family for cheering me on and making way for me to have time and energy to work on the manuscript. Thanks, Luke and Kenzie, for your patience and pitching in!

Most of all, thanks to my Blessed Mother who has been my constant companion and guide throughout.

NOTES

Introduction

1. Karin Vélez, *The Miraculous Flying House of Loreto: Spreading Catholicism in the Early Modern World* (Princeton, NJ: Princeton University Press, 2019), 3–5.

2. Michael O'Neill, "House of Loreto with Michael O'Neill," EWTN, May 31, 2022.

3. Ibid.

4. Vélez, *The Miraculous Flying House of Loreto*, 12–13.

5. Richard Klaver, OSC., *The Litany of Loreto* (St. Louis, MO: B. Herder Book Co., 1954), 1.

6. Ibid., 3.

7. Ibid.

8. Ibid., 11–12.

9. Ibid., 11.

10. Vélez, *The Miraculous Flying House of Loreto*, 206.

11. Ibid.

12. Klaver, *The Litany of Loreto*, 3–4.

13. Alexis M. Lépicier, OSM., *The Fairest Flower of Paradise: Considerations on the Litany of the Blessed Virgin, Enriched with Examples Drawn from the Lives of the Saints* (London: Benziger Brothers, 1922), 8.

Holy Mary

1. Ibid., 4–5.

2. Mark Alessio, "The Most Holy Name of Mary, Part I," Catholic Tradition, http://www.catholictradition.org/Mary/marys-name.htm.

Holy Mother of God

1. John N. D. Kelly, "Nestorius: Bishop of Constantinople,"

Britannica, https://www.britannica.com/biography/Nestorius.

2. Paul VI, *Maralis Cultus*, quoted in Enzo Lodi, "Solemnity of Mary, Mother of God," https://www.ewtn.com/catholicism/library/solemnity-of-mary-mother-of-god-5826.

Holy Virgin of Virgins

1. United States Conference of Catholic Bishops, *Catechism of the Catholic Church*, 2nd ed. (Libreria Editrice Vaticana, 1997), 507. Subsequent excerpts from the *Catechism* will be cited as "CCC" in the text.

Mother of Mercy

1. Alphonsus Liguori, *The Glories of Mary* (New York: P.J. Kenedy & Sons, 1888, re-typeset 2015, America Needs Fatima, 2021), 4.

2. Ibid.

3. M. Faustina Kowalska, *Divine Mercy in My Soul: Diary* (Stockbridge, MA: Marian Press, 1987), 330.

Mother of Divine Grace

1. Thomas Aquinas, *Summa Theologica* III, q. 7, a. 9, emphasis added.

2. Lépicier, *The Fairest Flower of Paradise*, 44–45.

Mother of Purity

1. Thomas Aquinas, *Summa Theologica* III, q. 37, a. 4.

2. John Henry Newman, *The Mystical Rose: Thoughts on the Blessed Virgin from the Writings of John Henry Cardinal Newman*, ed. Joseph Regina (New York: Scepter Publishers, 1996).

Mother Most Chaste

1. Ibid., 76.

Mother Inviolate

1. John Vianney, *The Little Catechism of the Curé of Ars: Selected Passage from the Writings of the Curé of Ars* (Charlotte, NC: TAN Books, 1951), 17.

2. Johann Roten, SM, "Old Testament Type of Mary," University of Dayton, https://udayton.edu/imri/mary/o/old-testament-types-of-mary.php.

Mother Undefiled

1. Pius IX, *Ineffabilis Deus,* 1854, Papal Encyclicals Online, https://www.papalencyclicals.net/pius09/p9ineff.htm.

Mother of Good Counsel

1. Fr. Jonathan Niehaus, *200 Questions about Schoenstatt,* (Schoenstatt Fathers, 2002), #13.

2. Liguori, *The Glories of Mary*, 499.

Mother of Our Creator

1. Lépicier, *The Fairest Flower of Paradise*, 84.

Mother of Our Savior

1. Louis de Montfort, *True Devotion to Mary: With Preparation for Total Consecration*, trans. Father Frederick William Faber, DD (Charlotte, NC: TAN Classics, 2010), 76.

Mother Most Prudent

1. Thomas Aquinas, *Summa Theologica* II.II, q. 47, a. 2, and a. 6.

2. Ibid., q. 47, a. 6.

Mother Most Venerable

1. de Montfort, *True Devotion to Mary*, 30.

2. Lépicier, *The Fairest Flower of Paradise*, 109.

Virgin Most Renowned

1. Ligouri, *The Glories of Mary.*

Virgin Most Powerful

1. Newman, *The Mystical Rose*, 124–125.

Virgin Most Merciful

1. Philippe de Champaigne, *The Annunciation*, 1644, oil on oak, 28x28 ¾ in. (71.1x73cm), Metropolitan Museum of Art, New York, https://www.metmuseum.org/art/collection/search/438724.

Virgin Most Faithful

1. Donald H. Calloway, MIC, *Consecration to St. Joseph: The Wonders of Our Spiritual Father* (Stockbridge, MA: Marian Press, 2020), 35.

Mirror of Justice

1. "Social Justice Ministry," Archdiocese of Milwaukee, https://www.archmil.org/offices/social-justice.htm.

Seat of Wisdom

1. "The Roman Catholic Shrine of Our Lady, the Slipper Chapel," Walsingham Village, https://www.walsinghamvillage.org/about/the-roman-catholic-shrine-slipper-chapel/.

2. "The Statue of Our Lady of Walsingham," The Catholic National Shrine and Basilica of Our Lady, https://www.walsingham.org.uk/the-statue-of-our-lady-of-walsingham/.

Mystical Rose

1. Margaret Rose Realy, Obl. OSB, *A Garden Catechism: 100 Plants in Christian Tradition and How to Grow Them* (Huntington, IN: Our Sunday Visitor, 2022), 222.

2. Newman, *The Mystical Rose*, 83–84.

Tower of David

1. "Tower of David — Where the History of Jerusalem Comes to Life," Israel Advantage Tours, https://israeladvantagetours.com/tower-of-david-where-the-history-of-jerusalem-comes-to-life/.

2. De Montfort, *True Devotion to Mary*, 23.

Tower of Ivory

1. Newman, *The Mystical Rose,* 118.

2. "Still poached for ivory," World Wildlife Fund, https://wwf.panda.org/discover/knowledge_hub/endangered_species/elephants/african_elephants/afelephants_threats.

Morning Star

1. Joe Rao, "What is a 'morning star,' and what is an 'evening star'?" Space.com, https://www.space.com/31851-what-is-morning-star-evening-star.html.

2. Newman, *The Mystical Rose*, 131.

Health of the Sick

1. Thérèse of Lisieux, *The Story of a Soul: The Autobiography of the Little Flower* (Charlotte, NC: TAN Classics, 2010), 36–37.

Refuge of Sinners

1. Liguori, *The Glories of Mary*, 29.

2. "Titles of Our Lady from the Litany of Loreto: Refuge of Sinners," https://www.salvemariaregina.info/SalveMariaRegina/SMR-171/Refuge.htm.

3. "What does the Bible say about refuge?" OpenBible.info, https://www.openbible.info/topics/refuge.

Solace of Migrants

1. "Pope adds three new invocations to the Litany of the Blessed Virgin Mary," Vatican News, June 20, 2020, https://www.vaticannews.va/en/pope/news/2020-06/pope-francis-loreto-litany-new-invocations.html.

2. Sister M. Danielle Peters, "Flight into Egypt," University of Dayton, https://udayton.edu/imri/mary/f/flight-into-egypt.php.

Comfort for the Afflicted

1. "Stabat Mater," Our Catholic Prayers, https://www.ourcatholicprayers.com/stabat-mater.html.

Help of Christians

1. Chris Mueller, "7 of the Greatest Hail Mary Passes of All Time," History, https://www.history.com/news/greatest-hail-mary-passes.

2. Paul Kengor, "Remembering the Battle of Lepanto: 450 Years Ago," EWTN, https://ewtn.co.uk/article-remembering-the-battle-of-lepanto-450-years-ago/.

Queen of Patriarchs

1. Philip Kosloski, "Who are the main patriarchs in the Bible?" Aleteia, https://aleteia.org/2019/09/26/who-are-the-main-patriarchs-in-the-bible/.

Queen of Martyrs

1. Marge Steinhage Fenelon, *My Queen, My Mother: A Marian Pilgrimage Across America* (Notre Dame, IN: Ave Maria Press, 2019), 85.

2. Ibid., 87–88.

3. Ibid.

Queen of Confessors

1. John Arthur Orr, "Reflection On: Queen of Confessors, Pray for Us," Ad Rationem, October 27, 2020, https://www.adrationem.com/2020/10/27/reflection-on-queen-of-confessors-pray-for-us/.

Queen of Virgins

1. Fulton J. Sheen, *The World's First Love: A Moving and Eloquent Portrayal of Mary, Mother of God.* (New York: Image Books, 1952).

2. "Meet the 7 women mentioned during the Eucharistic prayer at Mass," Aletia, https://aleteia.org/2018/03/18/meet-the-7-women-mentioned-during-the-eucharistic-prayer-at-mass/.

3. The Canon Law Society of America, *New Commentary on the Code of Canon Law,* ed. John P. Beal, James A. Coriden, and Thomas J. Green (Mahwah, NJ: Paulist Press, 2000), canon 604.

4. Sheen, *The World's First Love.*

Queen Conceived Without Original Sin

1. Aquinas, *Summa Theologiae* I.II, q. 81, a. 3.

2. Pius IX, *Ineffabilis Deus.*

Queen Assumed Into Heaven

1. "The Assumption of the Blessed Virgin Mary," EWTN https://www.ewtn.com/catholicism/saints/assumption-of-the-blessed-virgin-mary-814.

Queen of the Most Holy Rosary

1. "St. Dominic Receives the Rosary," Dominican Friars Foundation, https://dominicanfriars.org/st-dominic-receiving-rosary/.

2. Louis de Montfort, *The Secret of the Rosary*, trans. Mary Barbour, TOP (Bay Shore, NY: Montfort Publications, 1995), 1.

3. Ibid., 76–77.

Queen of Families

1. John Paul II, *Familiaris Consortio*, November 22, 1981, The Holy See, https://www.vatican.va/, 86.

Queen of Peace

1. John Arthur Orr, "Reflection On: Queen of Peace, Pray For Us," *Ad Rationem*, December 16, 2020, https://www.adrationem.com/2020/12/16/reflection-on-queen-of-peace-pray-for-us/,
2. Michael O'Neill, "The Messages of Fatima," The Miracle Hunter, https://www.miraclehunter.com/marian_apparitions/messages/fatima_messages.html.
3. Ibid.

Selected Bibliography

Calloway, Donald H., MIC. *Consecration to St. Joseph: The Wonders of Our Spiritual Father*. Marian Stockbridge, MA: Press, 2020.

De Montfort, Louis. *The Secret of the Rosary*. Translated by Mary Barbour, TOP. Bay Shore, NY: Montfort Publications, 1995.

———. *True Devotion to Mary: With Preparation for Total Consecration*. Translated by Father Frederick William Faber, D.D. Charlotte, NC: TAN Classics, 2010.

Dollen, Charles. *Listen, Mother of God! Reflections on the Litany of Loreto*. Huntington, IN: Our Sunday Visitor, 1989.

Dominican Sisters of Mary, Mother of the Eucharist. *Manual for Marian Devotion*. Charlotte, NC: Tan Books, 2016.

Lépicier, Alexis M., OSM. *The Fairest Flower of Paradise: Considerations on the Litany of the Blessed Virgin, Enriched with Examples Drawn from the Lives of the Saints*. London: Benziger Brothers, 1922.

Kowalska, M. Faustina. *Divine Mercy in My Soul: Diary*. Stockbridge, MA: Marian Press, 1987.

The Life of Mary as Seen by the Mystics. Compiled by Raphael Brown. Charlotte, NC: TAN Books, 2012.

Liguori, Alphonsus. *The Glories of Mary*. New York: P. J. Kenedy & Sons, 1888, re-typeset 2015, America Needs Fátima, 2021.

Newman, John Henry. *The Mystical Rose: Thoughts on the Blessed Virgin from the Writings of John Henry Cardinal Newman*. Edited by Joseph Regina. New York: Scepter Publishers, 1996.

Realy, Margaret Rose. *A Garden Catechism: 100 Plants in Christian Tradition and How to Grow Them*. Huntington, IN: Our Sunday Visitor, 2022.

Sheen, Fulton J. *The World's First Love: A Moving and Eloquent Portrayal of Mary, Mother of God*. New York: Image Books, 1952.

Thérèse of Lisieux. *The Story of a Soul: The Autobiography of the Little Flower*. Charlotte, NC: TAN Classics, 2010.